ADD-FRIENDLY
Ways To
ORGANIZE
Your Life

ADD-FRIENDLY
Ways To
ORGANIZE
Your Life

JUDITH KOLBERG and
KATHLEEN NADEAU, Ph.D.

Psychology Press
Taylor & Francis Group

New York   London

Published in 2002 by
Routledge
Taylor & Francis Group
711 Third Avenue
New York, NY 10017

Published in Great Britain by
Routledge
Taylor & Francis Group
2 Park Square
Milton Park, Abingdon
Oxon OX14 4RN

© 2002 by Judith Kolberg and Kathleen Nadeau
Routledge is an imprint of Taylor & Francis Group

Printed in the United States of America on acid-free paper

International Standard Book Number-10: 1-58391-358-0 (Softcover)
International Standard Book Number-13: 978-1-58391-358-1 (Softcover)
Library of Congress Card Number 2001052478

Note From The Authors: The authors have chosen to use the term ADD in this book because it is the term most widely used by the public to refer to the condition officially known as Attention Deficit/Hyperactivity Disorder (AD/HD). ADD refers to all variants of attention defiicit disorder, with or without hyperactivity.

Cover design: Jennifer Crisp

Library of Congress Cataloging-in-Publication Data

Kolberg, Judith
    ADD-friendly ways to organize your life / Judith Kolberg and Kathleen Nadeau.
        p. cm.
    Includes bibliographical references and index.
    ISBN 1-58391-358-0 (pbk. : alk. paper)
    1. Attention-deficit disorder in adults. 2. Management. 3. Organization.
    I. Nadeau, Kathleen G. II. Title.
RC394.A85 K653   2002
616.85'89—dc21   2001052478

Visit the Taylor & Francis Web site at
http://www.taylorandfrancis.com

and the Routledge Web site at
http://www.routledge.com

Contents

Foreword

On the day the manuscript for *ADD-Friendly Ways to Organize Your Life* arrived, I had just finished spending an hour with John, a generally well adjusted, vocationally successful adult with a history of ADD beginning in early childhood. A sibling of his had also been diagnosed with ADD. Despite struggling with ADD, John had managed to complete college, marry, have two children, and enter his father's business. At thirty-one years of age, John reports that he is happy and satisfied with life. He continues to take medication for his condition with benefit. He participates in intermittent counseling with me, focusing on specific work, family, and life issues as they arise.

John describes himself as a productive and reasonably well adjusted member of society. But as he notes, observers may not be able to read between the lines of his life. He is chronically disorganized at work and at home. He has a very difficult time completing tasks at hand without succumbing to tangential distractions. He finds it nearly impossible to complete simple, necessary tasks such as getting to work on time or following through with household responsibilities. His marriage is often strained to the breaking point due to his inability to focus during a conversation or respond to the needs of his spouse. When he finds something that piques his interest, all else gets pushed aside.

On this particular day for probably the fifth time, John and I spent a good part of the hour discussing how to best organize his office and possessions. Though we had tried a number of organizational techniques and strategies, many of which worked initially, John struggled to find the power to consistently stay the course. The techniques were effective, but the amount of self-control required was simply more than John could muster. So that day we decided to seek new strategies, ones that might be more compatible with the chronic nature of the ADD condition.

ADD is a condition affecting individuals differently but consistently throughout their life span. The research literature on this condition during the adult years—or, for that matter, on the risk factors related to this condition affecting adult outcome during the childhood years—is still very small in comparison to the body of research on ADD in general. Nonetheless, there is a consensus that the core symptoms of ADD affect a significant minority of the adult population. For affected individuals this condition represents a poor fit between society's expectations and their ability to meet these expectations.

ADD is distinct from other disorders of adulthood and can be reliably evaluated and effectively treated. Finally, this condition leads to a high financial cost to society when adults are unable to transition into functional life or even when, in adults such as John, the condition disrupts their careers or marriage. We recognize that the treatment for the symptoms and consequences of ADD must be multidisciplinary and must be maintained throughout the affected individual's life. Though the symptoms and consequences may wax and wane, there is no treatment leading to complete recovery, particularly given the complex demands of our current culture.

In *ADD-Friendly Ways to Organize Your Life*, Judith Kolberg and Kathleen Nadeau offer a practical and logical set of guidelines that are theoretically and scientifically compatible with ADD. They begin by helping the reader understand the nature of ADD and the insidious means by which this condition impairs the capacity to develop, maintain, and organize daily life. They offer a framework of interventions consistent with the impairments of this condition and compatible with current theory. Finally, their model is consistent with the current science of ADD, providing affected individuals with strategies to enhance consistent and predictable self-regulation in all aspects of daily life.

Rather than reflecting a problem with attention, ADD truly reflects a problem with self-regulation leading to impaired functioning in everyday life, in particular significant problems with planning, organization, and follow-through. Kolberg and Nadeau recognize the problems encountered by individuals with ADD when tasks are repetitive, effortful, uninteresting, and not necessarily chosen. They understand the need for reinforcement to be immediate, predictable, frequent, and meaningful.

ADD-Friendly Ways to Organize Your Life is a text that I will add to my very short list of recommended self-help volumes for adults with ADD who are interested in and capable of taking charge of their lives—and living more effectively. It is a work that I will refer to frequently.

Sam Goldstein, Ph.D.

Preface

This book was long in the making, and long overdue in responding to the needs of adults with attention deficit/hyperactivity disorder. It is one of the only books that deals directly and exclusively with the greatest challenge that adults with ADD face—the problem of disorganization.

Because it was originally thought that ADD was a disorder of childhood, and more particularly a disorder of boys, attention was paid primarily to the boyhood problems associated with attention disorders—having difficulty sitting down, being quiet, and paying attention. How to get young (mainly boys) with ADD to simply sit, listen, and behave (control themselves) was the primary concern.

As the years have passed, our knowledge of ADD has progressed. New insights have emerged. We now know that ADD affects many girls and women, and that females often struggle with issues different from those of males. We also know that ADD is a life-span disorder. It doesn't go away; it simply evolves as we grow older. As children with ADD grow into young adults and beyond, the expectation is no longer to simply "sit still and listen." It is to "take charge of your life." Taking charge requires learning to organize.

Being organized has never been more important. We must organize our time, our belongings, and our living and work space or we'll be overwhelmed by the flood of communications from the outside world. We receive more mail in one month than our parents received in a year and more mail in one year than our grandparents received in a lifetime. And that's not counting voice mail on our answering machines and e-mail on our computers. And the volume is still growing. We now have such easy access to our money through the ubiquitous ATMs that it takes more self-discipline to control impulse spending and consumption. The sheer quantity of paper and things that come into our life that must be organized is a challenge, even for people without ADD.

The increasingly complex number of choices in everyday life makes good decision-making skills essential, and organizing our time a must. Paper or plastic? Mutual funds or individual stocks? This daycare center or that one? Everywhere we turn, a decision must be made from among increasing choices. And he who hesitates is lost. Procrastination can result in being lost in mounting decisions, paper, clutter, and stress. Even time itself has changed. Everyone agrees that there simply seems to be less of it.

The appearance of twenty-four-hour grocery stores and gas stations has eliminated the natural rhythm to the twenty-four-hour cycle. In most European countries, there is still a culturally agreed-upon daily schedule, from which people rarely vary. Stores are open during limited hours, with little evening or weekend availability. Meals occur at standard hours, and for fairly standard lengths of time. But here in the United States, our options have opened up, requiring each of us to plan and prioritize more actively. We can eat, shop, fill up the car with gas, or obtain cash at any time of the day or night, during the week or on the weekend. We're forced to either create our own patterns or fall into unplanned chaos.

In the world of work, profound changes have occurred that strike hard upon the lives of adults with ADD. Many of the hands-on, physical jobs that have always existed in the past have been taken over by machines, leaving an abundance of jobs in the service, communication, and technology fields—jobs that require less physical activity and more mental concentration, more sustained focus on details, and more information to be classified and organized.

The great majority of adults not only commute longer to work, but are part of a dual-career couple, meaning that there is no spouse at home to order and organize the home and personal activities of the family while the other focuses on work demands. All of these factors combine, resulting in greater than ever challenges for adults with ADD. Stress is particularly high for women with ADD who are expected to have an organized home, organized children, and an organized life regardless of other demands on them.

As our understanding of ADD has progressed, so has our understanding of organization. Recognition of learning differences and disorders, appreciation for variations in attention spans, and new understandings of learning styles have all contributed to organizing advice and methods that are more effective than ever for people with ADD. In this book, we (Judith Kolberg, a professional organizer with a great sensitivity to the organizing needs of ADD adults and Kathleen Nadeau, a nationally recognized authority on adult ADD) join together in addressing the challenges faced by today's adults with ADD in a simple, straightforward fashion.

While other books on organizing have been written, none have been focused on the particular challenges and dilemmas of adults with ADD. We hope that our readers will find that this book can help them organize their life, allowing them to spend their energy focusing on their strengths rather than floundering in daily disorder.

Acknowledgments

Judith Kolberg:

I would like to acknowledge the contribution of my coauthor, Dr. Kathleen Nadeau. Kathleen's commitment to people with ADD never faltered and her vision to publish this book remained firm when I nearly lost confidence. People with ADD can take great pride in her talent and tenacity. My thanks go to Penny Walker, who helped with pulling the manuscript together, and to illustrators Stephen Sweny and Stephanie Troncalli. Thanks also to the National Study Group on Chronic Disorganization for the professional context in which to talk about ADD and organizing theory. I am grateful to all my ADD clients for the real world education they provided me. A special thanks to the many manufacturers and the associate members of the National Association of Professional Organizers who provided graphics for this book. Appreciated also are Sari Solden's and Sandra Felton's insights and those of many authors who understand the challenge that organizing is for people with ADD. Thanks to the women at EcoColors and Annemarie Poyo for making me look good. Finally, I would like to thank George Zimmar, Hope Breeman, and Barbara Michaluk for stepping in and grabbing the reins to make this the book it always had the potential to be.

Kathleen Nadeau:

First, I am grateful to the many adults with ADD with whom I've worked in therapy over the years. They have been my teachers sharing their struggles and triumphs along the path to taking charge of their lives. Many thanks to Judith Kolberg for her numerous suggestions, insights, and creative organizing solutions, not to mention her patience and perseverance in completing this project. Thanks to Hope Breeman and George Zimmar at Brunner-Routledge for their enthusiasm and patience as this book has come to fruition in a very unorthodox fashion. As always, kudos to Barbara Michaluk, with whom I've worked on numerous book projects, whose intimate understanding of ADD guides her in designing books that really work for people with ADD. And finally, a big hug to each of the members of my very interesting, very ADD family, from whom I've learned most of what I know about succeeding with ADD.

Part *One*

Getting Started

ADD-Friendly Organizing:
A Different Organizing Approach

For many adults with ADD, life feels overwhelming and chaotic. Their homes are cluttered; laundry and dishes go undone; unread newspapers and magazines pile up. Their cars are cluttered; mobile storage units are filled with a jumble of items—clothes to take to the cleaners, misplaced athletic shoes, and half-eaten, dried-out fast food. Time rushes by and they don't notice; bills and important paperwork are buried under piles. Their finances are often in overdraft; charge cards are up to their limits; frequent late fees are assessed; tax returns are filed late. When they make an effort to get organized, their clutter seems to magically reappear only minutes after it has been cleared away.

If you are an adult with ADD who struggles with organizing, this book was written with you in mind. Other organizing books often aren't helpful because their approaches aren't well designed for people with ADD. The advice may be too detailed. For example, other organizing books might suggest setting up a complex paper filing system when most adults with ADD would be thrilled simply to see the surface of their dining room table again. Or, there is an assumption that readers will be able to put their home or office in order, based on a book's suggestions, without any other support.

You've probably tried to "get organized" many times before—buying organizing books, day planners, software, and electronic gadgets—but nothing in the past has worked. You start out with the best intentions, only to find that each new organizing system falls apart very quickly. This doesn't mean that getting organized is a hopeless quest, but it does mean that you need special approaches designed for adults with ADD. That's what this book offers, ADD-friendly ways to organize your life. In this book, you'll find stories about adults with ADD, describing the organizing dilemmas they've encountered and the ADD-friendly approaches that worked for them—and that may work for you as well.

Dr. Nadeau

Problems with planning and organization are among the biggest challenges for adults with ADD. This is especially true for women, who are often expected to organize not only themselves, but their family as well.

How is this book different?

- It's written by two experts: an expert on ADD, Kathleen Nadeau, Ph.D., and an expert on organizing, Judith Kolberg.

- The tips and tools in this book are specifically designed for adults with ADD.

- Not only is our advice ADD-friendly, but the book's format is ADD-friendly too, with clear topics, bold headings, readable print, an open page design, and a reader-friendly writing style.

Years ago, I began to realize that most organizing tools and training didn't work well for most adults with ADD. For example, day-long seminars on time management or organization require people to listen effectively for six to eight hours at a time. Listening for that long is difficult for most people, and next to impossible for adults with ADD. Also, most organizing books and seminars assume that you will be able to put their organizing ideas into action on your own, without structure or support—the "just do it" school of organizing. If it were that simple, adults with ADD would have gotten organized long ago!

On top of unrealistic expectations, many suggested organizing approaches themselves are ludicrously inappropriate for adults with

ADD. Someone whose garage resembles a landfill, or whose dining room table is permanently covered with piles of papers, isn't likely to benefit from detailed advice on record-keeping or filing systems.

Other organizing systems don't take into account the ADD stumbling blocks of inconsistency and forgetfulness. For example, dayplanners and personal digital assistants, very popular organizing tools, are extremely helpful for many adults, and can be helpful for adults with ADD as well. However, without learning strategies to counteract the inconsistency and forgetfulness so often associated with ADD, these tools can't be used effectively.

To use a planner successfully, you must first learn to use it consistently—to write necessary information about schedules and tasks in the planner on a daily basis, and to consult their planner regularly throughout the day. And even those adults with ADD who enter information and consult their planner on a daily basis must also develop strategies to keep their planner with them at all times, and to avoid misplacing or losing it. The standard training seminars on the use of day planners don't even begin to address these typical ADD challenges.

After repeated failed efforts to take charge of your life, you may be convinced that the task is impossible. Instead, the problem may lie in the approaches that you've tried. In this book, we'll help you learn to better understand yourself and how you are affected by ADD, so that you can develop successful strategies to manage the organizing tasks of your life. The keys to ADD-friendly organizing success involve:

- **S**trategies (ADD-friendly strategies, of course!);
- **S**upport; and
- **S**tructure.

We'll come back to these "three S's" again and again throughout the book, as we describe ADD-friendly organizing approaches.

Judith Kolberg

The difference between the organizing needs of people without ADD, and those of people with ADD, could not have been more apparent to me than when I began to do organizing work with "Olivia." What an education! Olivia is a mini-whirlwind, a swirl of dangling purses, bags of groceries, car keys, and odd papers. Always in motion (mainly because she is often late and hurrying), Olivia whirls to answer the phone, spins around to yell out to the children, frees a hand to pet the dog as she simultaneously opens the door. Her desk and dining room table are buried beneath unopened mail, newspapers, and loose papers. "I tend to disorganize spontaneously," she explains. It's true. I watch her turn a clear space on the kitchen counter into a clump of clutter in no time at all.

I am a good professional organizer. Olivia is a successful career woman. With patience and a can-do attitude, I figure we can organize Olivia's life. But few of the approaches I used with other adults seem to work for Olivia. I try putting her papers in file folders with titles, stacking them neatly in her in-box. But Olivia can't find anything. Two weeks later, her desk is overflowing again with heaps of papers. I teach her the time-honored, "A place for everything and everything in its place" proverb as we put things away and try to clear out the clutter. But these approaches are thwarted by her forgetfulness. She leaves her cell phone behind, and the dog's leash is no where to be found. We work on her time-management skills. With my support, Olivia agrees to plan her week in advance, on paper; however, her plans deteriorate into a rush of semi-emergencies and unplanned surprises.

Eventually Olivia explained to me that she had attention deficit disorder. At first I was convinced that even a neurologically based organic disorder like ADD would eventually yield to the logic of standard organizing approaches. What I learned, though, was that these standard approaches couldn't work for Olivia—and don't work for many others with ADD.

Here's what *did* work. Instead of filing papers in plain old manila file folders assembled into a filing cabinet, we bought a colorful milk crate and stuck casters (wheels) on it. Inside we used multicolored file folders with lettering on the tabs, and instead of using many file folders, her papers were filed into a few simple categories. Everything was easy to see and simple to retrieve. Olivia learned to develop the habit of filing a little every day instead of letting it accumulate into a big, overwhelming stack. Then, she simply tucked the filing crate underneath the dining room table.

We liberated the dining room table from the tons of junk mail that had imprisoned it. This was accomplished by turning on some of Olivia's favorite music and teaming her up with a "clutter companion." Simply a friend, and not a critic, Olivia's clutter companion provided moral support and another set of hands while she kept her on task. To counteract some of her forgetfulness, we had a good time putting up reminder signs in logical spots like on the door, on the bathroom mirror, and in the car. And we learned to be more realistic. Maybe Olivia wasn't quite ready to plan an entire week at a time. We planned a day at a time instead, until she got the hang of managing her time realistically. Then we moved on to planning a week.

Many of the approaches suggested in this book were developed through my work with Olivia and others with ADD. They speak directly to the organizing issues people with ADD confront: distractibility, variations in attentiveness, hyperfocus, and stimulation issues. Like Olivia, by learning ADD-friendly approaches, you can organize your life. It just takes a different perspective, one with more creativity, more support and structure, and less self-criticism!

Organizing your life is a custom-ordered task. Although all of the strategies we describe are designed with the ADD adult in mind, not every approach suggested in this book will be a good fit for you. As you read this book, select and adapt those approaches that best match your lifestyle and temperament.

Start with the most basic and important ADD-friendly organizing concept:

**Don't fight *against* your ADD;
work *with* your ADD to
take charge of your life.**

In the following chapters, we'll teach you ways to do just that.

Review

■ Standard organizing approaches often don't work for adults with ADD.

■ Organizing techniques that work are those that help you compensate for your ADD-related struggles such as forgetfulness, distractibility, and difficulties with time management.

■ Your best organizing strategy is to work *with* your ADD instead of fighting against it.

■ The "Three S's"—*strategies, support,* and *structure*—are the keys to ADD organizing success.

Chapter Two

ADD-Friendly Strategies
That Work *with* Your ADD

If you're like many adults with ADD, you put "getting organized" on your list of odious and impossible tasks—like a starvation weight-loss regime, or a predawn daily exercise plan—something requiring iron will and perseverance. There may be a person in your life who seems to embody all the organizing virtues—"early to bed, early to rise," combined with "a place for everything and everything in its place." Modeling your behavior after someone who is very controlled, perhaps over-controlled, can rarely work if you're an adult with ADD. Those few adults with ADD who are super-organized typically consume every waking moment in their organizing efforts.

Work *with* Your ADD to Get Organized

"Shoulds" and "oughts" rarely motivate adults with ADD in the long run. To stay motivated, you need something that will focus your attention, engage your interest, and stimulate you.

> **If you want to get organized,**
> **get *focused, engaged, and stimulated!***

This book will teach you how to work *with* your ADD to take charge of your life. Following are some techniques to get "hooked" on ADD-friendly organizing.

Make It Fun

Think it's impossible to have fun while decluttering? Think again! Get the whole family involved. Competition often makes things more interesting. For example, give everyone a "five-minute challenge." Set a timer for five minutes. The game is for each player to enter his or her bedroom and spend five minutes stuffing items into a bag to throw away or a give away.

The person who gathers the most *appropriate* items in a five-minute period wins the round. We insert the word appropriate because some children may become carried away, and may indiscriminately stuff items into the bag, including perfectly good items of clothing, game parts, or school supplies.

Five minutes is painless, and this can be a daily event until rooms are cleared out—with a special dessert or other small prize going to each day's winner.

> **To get it done, make it fun!**

Catch the Mood

Adults with ADD can catch a mood and ride it as effortlessly as some surfers catch a wave. Working *with* your mood often works better for adults with ADD than trying to schedule a task. Being in the mood to organize may catch you by surprise. You may be looking in the back of the closet for your snow boots, and, before you know it, you're madly tossing galoshes, mismatched gloves, and old winter jackets out into the hallway.

Impulses can lead either to chaos or decluttering depending upon how you handle them. Chaos ensues if you leave the mess in the hallway, only to later toss it all back, pell-mell, into the closet. But significant decluttering can take place if you organize yourself just a bit—long enough to grab a throw-away and a give-away bag, toss the items inside one or the other, and haul the bags to the garage or other storage space awaiting trash day or pick-up days scheduled by your local charity.

Organize for Reasons That Matter to You

Don't try to adopt someone else's organizing values. If being "tidy" or "organized" has negative connotations for you (tedious, boring, uptight, perfectionist), motivate yourself by organizing according to your own values.

For example, if you value social service, put together coordinated outfits from clothing that you want to discard, then donate these complete outfits to a local homeless shelter or shelter for victims of domestic abuse. Your castoffs can be transformed into job-interview outfits for women with limited income. With this goal in mind, you're not engaged in tedious tidying—you're making a positive difference in the life of someone less fortunate.

If you value creativity, imagine an art project—a collage, a quilt, a sculpture, or braided rug. Then, just as some artists collect objects at the local dump, or collect discarded clothing at a thrift store for their art projects, go around the house with a collection bag looking for items for future art projects. You've had fun collecting materials and have decluttered your environment at the same time.

To Get Organized, Get Energized!

Many adults with ADD can move from a couch potato state to one of high energy in response to the right kind of stimulation. Think about what stimulates you best. For some it's physical movement. For others it's companionship. Singing can make time melt while you're engaged in uninteresting chores. Lively music is often a good motivator. You may need to create a beehive of activity to get motivated and stay motivated while you organize.

Divide the Dreadful into Micro-moments

If the activity is something you truly dread, divide the activity into micro-moments. For example, if you detest filing or processing papers, set a low limit for each filing exercise. Decide that each time you enter your office (at home or at work) that you will process the first ten paper items that you happen to pick up. Some you may immediately toss, others you may need to file, still others require that you complete a form or write a check. If you're lucky enough to grab ten papers that can be tossed you'll be done in seconds! Rarely should you need to process papers for more than ten or fifteen minutes if you use this rule. You'll be amazed how quickly the paper chaos melts when you use this micro-moment approach to drudgery.

Take Advantage of Organizational Moments

Organizational moments are times when you take advantage of unplanned opportunities to organize. An example is filing a paid bill and then, while you're at it, flipping through the file folder and throwing out any obsolete junk. Or it might be taking the opportunity to empty out your glove compartment when you're stopped at a traffic signal. Or cleaning out your purse while you search for your nail file buried at the bottom.

Think like a Restaurant Server

Many restaurant servers have ADD tendencies and are attracted to the work because it is active, social, and allows them to maintain their long-established night-owl tendencies. Think like a restaurant server when you're in your own environment. A busy restaurant never allows the tables to remain cluttered. Dishes are quickly removed as soon as a menu item is eaten. A server is constantly in the process of decluttering and reorganizing. Have you ever watched a restaurant table cleared and reset? The table is wiped, new table cloth put down, salt, pepper, flower vase, whatever items that belong on the table are instantly reorganized so that the table looks fresh for the next set of diners.

A server learns that creating clutter (by serving diners) and removing clutter (by taking plates away) is one integrated process.

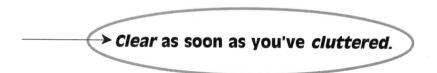

➤ _Clear_ as soon as you've _cluttered._

When you think like a server at home, you get into the habit of tidying as you go. Hang up the robe on the hook as you leave your bedroom. Scan each room for cups or glasses as you pass from one room to the next, and automatically take them to the kitchen.

So often our clutter gets the best of us because we think of "straightening up" as a separate, distinct, and dreaded activity that we put off as long as possible.

Be a Sprinter, Not a Long-Distance Runner

Remember the old story of the tortoise and the hare, whose moral is that "slow and steady wins the race"? That story was obviously written by a tortoise! If you have ADD, you'll operate better as a hare, going as fast as you can to the finish line. The key is to make the race short, so that you'll be able to cross the finish line without stopping. For ADD-friendly organizing, be a sprinter, not a long-distance runner.

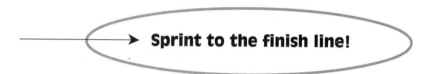

➤ Sprint to the finish line!

In practical terms, being a sprinter means dividing up organizing projects into small pieces that can be completed, from start to finish, in one dash. That way, you're less likely to be interrupted, to tire of the project, or to become distracted. Sprinting is stimulating, and keeps your interest high. No matter how large the organizing project, it can be broken down into short sprints.

ADD Patterns and Disorganization

In the preceding paragraphs, we've described ways to work *with* your ADD to organize. It's equally important to recognize common ADD patterns that lead to disorganization. Then you can learn strategies to counteract those patterns.

Heading "EAST"

People with ADD often head "EAST," trying to do everything at the same time (EAST). They may begin multiple organizing projects with great enthusiasm—purchasing storage boxes, shelving, and paint but months later, the shelving hasn't been taken out of the boxes and the paint cans are still unopened. To change this self-defeating habit, remember:

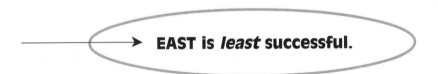

EAST is *least* successful.

In your enthusiasm, you overextend yourself in the beginning, and then complete few if any of the projects that you started. Instead, it's better to:

Choose just one, then get it done.

ADD-Friendly Strategies

Getting off Track

ADD brains tend to be reactive—that is, they react to whatever comes into their immediate vicinity—making it harder for adults with ADD to stay on track with projects. "Sprinting to the finish line" is one ADD-friendly approach to stay on track—by not giving yourself a chance to dawdle and look at other things. Another ADD-friendly approach to staying on track is to have a "body double" in the room. We'll talk more about this in the next chapter, but basically, a body double is someone who simply hangs out with you as you do your organizing task—to make sure you stay on task. With the added structure of another person in the room, you're less likely to start a diversionary tactic—such as starting to read a magazine article that you come across in your organizing efforts.

Use self-talk to stay on track.

If there's no one else to provide structure for you, self-talk can help. For example, use a kitchen timer when you're engaged in your organizing task. Set it repeatedly at ten-minute intervals. Each time it goes off, ask yourself, "Am I doing what I'm supposed to be doing?" If so, congratulations! If not, reset the timer and get yourself back on track.

Going into Micro-Focus

Adults with ADD often tend to slip into micro-focus when they're organizing—they get lost in the details instead of focusing on the larger task. For example, if your task is to declutter your family room, but you find yourself organizing photos in your photo album you've slipped into micro-focus, instead of keeping your focus on the "macro" task of clearing the family room. Going into micro-focus is often tempting for adults with ADD because it allows them to block out the "overwhelm" they feel when dealing with macro issues such as a large, clutter-filled room. Levels of focus—from macro to micro—will be discussed in detail later. A body double can help you avoid micro-focus, just as they can help you stay on track.

Underestimating

One of the effects of ADD is often a poor sense of time. Typically, adults with ADD grossly underestimate the amount of time a task will require. If you lose track of time, this can negatively impact others in your life who may be expecting you to meet them, or to meet another commitment.

To combat your poor time sense, instead of saying, "My goal is to clear out and organize the family room," set your goal in terms of time expenditure. For example, set a timer for one hour (or six ten-minute intervals if you tend to slip into micro-focus), and stop working at that point.

Getting Stuck

Adults with ADD seem to both underdo it and overdo it, as paradoxical as this seems. Underdoing occurs when we don't stick to a task we've set for ourselves because we're drawn away by something more interesting. Overdoing can also cause significant problems, and is related to a well-known ADD tendency to "get stuck" and resist moving on to the next task of the day. Staying stuck on one task can lead to other organizing challenges—you may be spending too much time on your current task at the expense of others. For example, spending hours on the computer designing a business card or brochure, while ignoring the undone dishes and laundry. Setting a time limit rather than a task limit can help avoid getting stuck.

Overcomplicating

Another ADD-related pattern that may interfere with organizing is to complicate a task. For example, you might decide to install a time management program on your computer—a potentially very useful approach to making better use of your time. However, if you're like many other adults with ADD, you might find that you've spent hours on your computer, customizing calendars, color-coding time blocks, and programming reminders—time that could have been better spent on another task. By making it overly complicated, you don't get down to the actual organizing.

ADD-Friendly Strategies

To get it done, keep it simple.

Adding without Subtracting

Adults with ADD often add things to their life—objects, activities, commitments—without doing the necessary subtraction. That's how ADD lives become so jam-packed—closets are packed with unworn clothing, bookshelves packed with unread books, schedules are packed with too many activities. All this addition increases the chronic stress in the lives of many adults with ADD. Many adults repeatedly convince themselves that they'll "find the time," or "make the room" for their latest addition, despite all the evidence to the contrary.

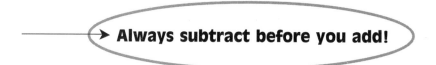

Always subtract before you add!

If you struggle with too much addition and too little subtraction, you may need to set very structured limits for yourself. To limit the addition of commitments, make a rule for yourself that you will not add a new commitment until you either finish or eliminate a prior commitment. Similar rules can be helpful for reading material (no new books or magazines until I read and/or give away unread books or magazines), or purchases (for every new article of clothing, at least two rarely worn articles will be put in the give-away bag).

As you begin to explore this book, remember:

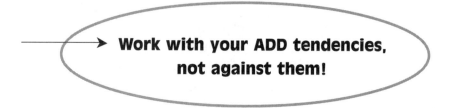

Work with your ADD tendencies, not against them!

Learning to organize in ADD-friendly ways is your key to success.

Review

■ If you want to get organized, get focused, engaged, and stimulated!

■ Make it fun!

■ Catch the mood.

■ Organize for reasons that matter to you.

■ Get energized to get organized!

■ Divide the "dreadful" into micro-moments.

■ Think like a restaurant server.

■ Sprint to the finish line!

■ EAST (everything at the same time) is *least* successful.

■ Learn to avoid:

   ■ overcomplicating;

   ■ underestimating;

   ■ getting off track;

   ■ getting stuck; and

   ■ going into micro-focus.

■ If you want to "add," you must learn to "subtract."

Chapter Three

Structure and Support: Creating the Framework for Success

In the preceding chapter, many ADD-friendly organizing strategies are introduced. But without *structure* and *support,* those strategies are less likely to be successful. With structure and support, you create the underlying framework for organizing success, a framework that will help you implement ADD-friendly strategies in a *consistent* and *persistent* manner. Think of these three "S's"—structure, support, and strategies—as a pyramid, with structure and support at the base.

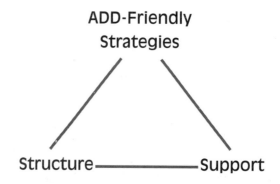

Structure and support can be introduced at different levels, depending upon how challenging the organizing task is for you.

Throughout the rest of this book, ADD-friendly strategies or solutions are suggested following each ADD organizing challenge. These solutions all involve structure and support. At **Level One,** we describe structure and support that you can provide yourself. At **Level Two**, we suggest a higher level of structure and support that can be provided by family and friends. At **Level Three**, we suggest strategies and solutions that involve professional assistance from professional organizers or ADD coaches. In some cases, the strategies we suggest may be ones that can be implemented at any level of support.

Match the Level of Support to the Challenge of the Task

For simpler organizing challenges, you may want to start with the lowest level of support that you can provide for yourself. For moderately challenging organizing tasks, you may decide to enlist friends or family members to provide structure and support. Some of your organizing challenges may feel so overwhelming that you'll elect to engage the support of a professional from the outset. Of course, as you learn techniques and build habits you may be able to reduce the level of support that you need to maintain organization.

Level 1: Creating Your Own Structure and Support

When you choose to organize independently you still need to think in terms of creating structure and support for each organizing challenge.

Structure

You can structure yourself in a variety of ways:

- **Create a schedule.** (From now on, I'll do my laundry every Saturday, rather than waiting until I have no clean clothes to wear.)

- **Break down the task into do-able bits.** (Instead of tackling my entire closet, I'll just organize these two shelves today.)

Structure and Support

19

▪ **Establish a step-by-step plan.** (This weekend, I'll purchase the shelving for my home office. Next weekend, mount the shelves and after that I'll use the shelves to neatly store the books and periodicals piled on the floor around my desk.

▪ **Develop habits and routines.** (A habit or routine is, by definition, structured—an activity that you do in a certain sequence at a certain time.)

ADD-Friendly Habit Building

If you're like many other adults with ADD, you've always had difficulty developing habits. Probably, when you've consciously tried to build a habit, you've gone about it in an ADD-*un*friendly way. For example, if you want to change your bedtime habits, it would be very ADD-*un*friendly to simply get into bed at 11 P.M. and turn out the light, willing yourself to go to sleep when your standard bedtime has been 2 A.M. for years. An ADD-friendly approach to changing your bedtime needs to involve a number of things.

▪ First, you may need to *change your evening routine* so that you have at least an hour to relax and calm down before turning out the light.

▪ Second, because our bodies become programmed to sleep and eat at certain times, you'll be more successful in getting to sleep earlier if you *move your bedtime earlier by twenty minute increments.* In that way, every three days you'll be turning the light out an hour earlier, so by day nine, you'll have a much greater chance of getting to sleep by 11 P.M.

▪ Third, you may need to *give up night-owl habits on weekends* to achieve your goal during the week. If you stay up until 2 or 3 A.M. on Saturday night each week, you've reset your biological clock back to the old pattern.

▪ Fourth, you may need to *introduce other supports* into your life to achieve your goal—such as an "artificial dawn" device that slowly lights your bedroom at a preprogrammed time each morning to help you get up, or a relaxing meditation tape to listen to as you fall asleep at night.

■ Fifth, you may find that your time awareness is so poor during the evening that, despite your best intentions, you stay up later than you intended. You may need to *set a reminder alarm,* or ask your partner or a family member to remind you when it's 10 P.M. and time to *begin your bedtime routine.*

We've chosen sleep habits, one of the most difficult habits to change for most adults with ADD, as our example. Other habits aren't so difficult to change, and may not require as much structure and support to achieve. However, this discussion of changing sleep habits is a good way to introduce the concept of ADD-friendly approaches to changing and building habits. The "just do it" approach to habit change rarely works for adults with ADD. Create the structure and support you need for each habit change and your chances for success are strong.

→ **"Just do it" doesn't get it done!**

Habit building is a powerful way to introduce structure into organizing—especially *maintenance* organizing. Maintenance organizing is the type of organizing that we all need to do on a regular, routine basis in order to maintain organization once it has been established. A professional organizer may help you work wonders in your environment. But without maintenance organizing, your new orderly environment will rapidly devolve into chaos again. That's because old habits remain firmly ingrained.

New habits take time. Don't be discouraged if you're not successful at first. Following are ten steps that make habit building successful for people with ADD. Just like all of the other organizing approaches that we suggest, you may find that you need support from others when you're in the early stages of habit building. Working with an ADD coach or professional organizer, who can help you stay on track as you build new habits, can be very effective.

Structure and Support

10 Steps to ADD-Friendly Habit Building

1. **Tie a new habit to an old one**. Most of us have some ingrained habits. It's easiest to develop a new one if it's tied to an old one. For example, place your vitamins next to your tooth brush to better remember to take your vitamins each morning.

2. **Make the habit as easy as possible**. For example, pick a convenient, visible place to put your keys, a place that makes sense, such as by the door you leave the house from.

3. **Make the habit hard to ignore.** Put bells on it, put it in a place where you'll trip over it, make it impossible to leave the house without it (tie your car keys to it).

4. **Put reminders everywhere**. When you are first starting out, put sticky notes where you are sure to see them that remind you to act on your new habit.

5. **Visualize yourself doing the new behavior.** For example, if this is a morning habit, imagine yourself going through your morning routine, including your new habit at the appropriate point in the routine.

6. **Practice "instant corrections."** If you forget to practice the new habit, go and do it the *instant* you remember it, if at all possible, even if it's not convenient.

7. **Get back on the horse and ride.** Habits take time; forgetting is *not* failure. It is part of developing a habit.

8. **Problem-solve if it's not working.** Maybe you need a different reminder. Perhaps you need to tie it to a different habit. Perhaps it would fit better into a different time of day.

9. **Practice the habit for at least thirty days in a row.** Make a calendar in the kitchen and check off the days.

10. **Reward yourself.** Celebrate when you reach your thirty-day goal.

Support

You can support yourself in many ways as you organize:

■ **Set *reasonable* goals**—avoid perfectionism.

■ **Use positive self-affirmations**—replace critical, negative messages in your head with encouraging ones.

■ **Recognize your progress**—instead of always focusing on the disorganization that remains to be tackled.

Organize for yourself, not for the approval of others

Many adults with ADD, especially women, approach organizing with feelings of failure and shame—failure to meet their mother's standards, their spouse's standards, society's standards, or standards they imagine are expected by others. It's important to define organization realistically. Your goal should be to meet your own needs, to create an environment that works for you, one that feels good to inhabit. You may need to examine more than once whether you are measuring your success against some external "should" instead of your own desires.

Be open to fresh ideas

Supporting your own organizing efforts also means trying new ideas and not doing the same old things over and over again. If you've tried to file papers in file folders and failed, give it up and try something different. If you can't use a to-do list, there are alternatives. This book gives you many fresh, new ideas. Look for something you have not yet tried even if it seems a little unusual to you. Have some fun. Break out of old patterns that don't work for you.

Level 2: Structure and Support from Friends and Family

One of the biggest struggles for an adult with ADD is to admit that he or she needs help—perhaps more help, more often than some other adults may need. Coming to terms with this may be difficult at first. You may tell yourself, "I'm smart, I'm capable. Cleaning, doing laundry, sorting, and organizing aren't rocket science. I don't need help. I just need to *decide* to do it." The challenge is that distractible ADD brains have difficulty staying on task, especially on mundane, uninteresting life-maintenance tasks. Adults with ADD also have more difficulty with unstructured tasks such as household maintenance. Women with ADD, especially, may have trouble admitting and accepting that such tasks are not their strong suit. Society puts subtle and not-so-subtle pressure upon women to take major roles, at home and in the workplace, in creating and maintaining order.

Give Yourself Permission to Get the Help You Need

Sari Solden, in her book *Women with Attention Deficit Disorder*, writes extensively about the ADD-unfriendly demands placed on many women, and encourages women with ADD to give themselves permission to obtain the help they need.

> Expand your idea of organizational help to include other people to help you. You need to get over the obsession with being an organized person or trying to "keep it together" in the same way non-ADD people do. A disorder means something is not of average difficulty and you might need a higher level of organizational support than other people. (p. 208)

Once an adult with ADD gives himself or herself permission to ask for help, half the battle has been won. Although you may prefer to begin with independent organizing strategies, if you find that your solo efforts are not successful, then it's time to build in more structure and support by engaging the help of family members or friends.

Benefits of Help from Friends and Family:

▮ Your morale will be higher.

▮ You won't be as distracted.

▮ You'll organize faster.

▮ You'll stay at it longer.

Working with Family Members

Family support can be very powerful when tackling major organizing challenges. For example, one family, in which both husband and wife had ADD traits, played "hot potato" for years, tossing recriminations back and forth, each claiming the other was primarily to blame for the chronic disorganization of their home. When they finally decided to join forces to attack their disorder, the mutual structure and support allowed them to make headway on tasks they had each avoided for years. Instead of assigning blame, they began to look for solutions. Instead of avoiding each other and the tasks at hand, they began to make "organizing appointments" with one another. As they came to recognize their need for structure, they began to interact differently with their children regarding chores, introducing schedules, structure, and support for them as well. Nagging and resentment decreased, while encouragement and camaraderie lightened the load. They had changed from an ADD-challenged family to an ADD-friendly family.

ADD-Friendly family organizing

■ **Let your family know specifically how your ADD affects you:** your ability to organize, your time management difficulties, your difficulty with follow-through, or problems in keeping track of things. The more your family understands ADD, the better they'll understand the reasons underlying your disorganization. Then, instead of blaming and criticizing, they can join you in finding solutions that work.

■ **Don't use ADD as an excuse.** Make it clear that you are working to improve your organization and that you need their help.

■ **Share information with your family**—the ideas, books, methods, or organizing advice you are following—so that they know what it is you are attempting to achieve.

■ If other family members face organizing challenges too, **make it a joint project to develop better organizing habits together.**

■ **Family members often make the best "maintenance organizers."** Once you've organized a closet, kitchen, or garage, family members can be great at helping you maintain your organizing effort. When you are disorganized, it's hard for other people, even well-intentioned people, to know how you want things or where to put things. But when you are organized, you have a system that your family can more easily help you to maintain.

Structure and Support from Friends

Friends can play a very constructive role as organizing support. They are less invested in your organizing progress than your family is and can be more objective and less judgmental. A friend can keep your morale up and help the work go faster, making the organizing work more satisfying. Having the support of a friend while you're organizing is not only warm and fuzzy, it is also very useful in counteracting distraction, one of your key concerns.

Many adults with ADD find that another adult with ADD can provide the best structure and support of all—support that can be reciprocal. (Help me dig out my kitchen this week, and I'll come over and help you next week.) But even when your friend does not have ADD, help can be reciprocal. For example, one man with ADD bartered technical computer support to a friend in exchange for assistance with organizing and tracking his financial records.

Organizing Roles that Family and Friends Can Play

Choose a support person who is patient, supportive, noncritical, and understanding of the organizing challenges that are part of having ADD. Ideally, they will bring enthusiasm and a sense of humor to the task. These can even be other people with ADD. Often, though they can't focus alone on their own organizing tasks, they can be focused and helpful when it's *your* stuff that's being organized. Friends or family can play a number of different support roles, Clutter Companion, Paper Partner, or Body Double.

If you have friends and family that fit into the roles of clutter companion, paper partner, time tutor, and body double, that would be ideal. These do not have to be four separate individuals. Perhaps you know someone in your family or among your friends who is great organizing papers *and* residential cutter. This one individual can perform the dual roles of clutter companion and paper partner. And remember this important fact: if you come up short on any of these roles, a professional organizer can step in to perform any of them.

To help guide you through areas of organizing that might be accomplished best with the support of a clutter companion, paper partner, time tutor, or body double, we've added a small picture of each everywhere they occur in the text.

Clutter Companion

Clutter Companion. Choose someone who is good at organizing possessions, clutter, closets, and storage areas in the home as your clutter companion.

Paper Partner

Paper Partner. For your paper partner, look for someone who is strong on organizing papers and filing.

Time Tutor

Time Tutor. Your time tutor should be someone who gets to places on time, seems to have a reasonable schedule, and accomplishes pretty much what they need to in the course of a day.

Body Double

Body Double. Sometimes all you need is the presence of someone else—a body double—in order to start organizing and keep organizing. A body double doesn't have to do anything but keep you company while you organize. Their presence is a support and a reminder that you are there to focus on a particular organizing task.

Level 3: Structure and Support from Professionals

There are many benefits to using a professional for support in getting organized. Professionals are skilled and objective. They have a great deal of experience helping adults with similar organizing challenges. Although family and friends can be helpful, their time and/or motivation may have limits. Family and friends may also not be objective because they are impacted by your organizing difficulties and may sometimes feel annoyed and frustrated with you.

There are several different approaches to organizing challenges that can be provided by professional organizers, ADD coaches, and psychotherapists who specialize in working with adults with ADD. You will need to decide which approach and what level of help will benefit you the most.

Professional Organizers

Sometimes adults with ADD need a level of support more intensive than family, friends, or coworkers can provide. A professional organizer (PO) provides hands-on help. Sometimes the support of a professional organizer at your side is what you need to get started, especially when the level of clutter feels overwhelming.

Later, when clutter has been reduced and storage shelves and containers are in place, the adult with ADD can begin to implement new habits and make decisions that will prevent the return of complete disorder. The needs of each adult differ. Some may need periodic "dig-outs" with a professional organizer; others can get support from family or friends to do maintenance tasks once a professional organizer has helped to create an ordered environment.

The kinds of services available from professional organizers include:

- helping to create solutions custom-designed to work for *you;*
- providing hands-on support as you implement these solutions; and
- helping you to select products and services to enhance your organization.

The attitude of an organizer is just as important as the practical solutions they suggest. A good organizer is encouraging, supportive, and nonjudgmental. No matter how big your mess, they've seen worse! The presence of an organizer can help you overcome your procrastination and reach decisions more quickly as you decide to give away, throw away, or store your belongings and papers. Most important, an organizer is respectful of your feelings and should never insist that you rid yourself of objects that you want to keep.

Choosing a professional organizer

The process of hiring a professional organizer is similar to that of choosing any consultant or independent contractor. You should ask:

- How long they have been in business?
- What is their area(s) of expertise?

■ Do they have experience with ADD?

■ Do they have references you can contact?

Sometimes you can tell from an initial phone call if the PO is someone you would feel comfortable working with, but often it takes one or two organizing sessions to determine if you've found a good match.

Not all professional organizers are good at working with adults with ADD. It's critical, if you decide to work with an organizer, that you find one who is very experienced and comfortable working with ADD issues.

ADD Coaches

An ADD coach offers a different kind of organizational support. Coaching can be very effective in helping you to build and maintain habits, to set goals and stay on track as you work toward them. A coach typically works by telephone (although your first contact may be in person), and you may have periodic in-person meetings with a coach.

While a professional organizer can work with you on-site, providing hands-on help to get your desk cleared off, a coach may be most effective in helping you to develop the habits that will *keep* your desk cleared off, once order has been established.

A coach can help you:

■ Analyze daily habits that create disorder. Do you leave unfinished projects on your desk top? When you've completed a task, do you fail to file papers away before you move on to the next task? Do you avoid filing and simply start piling again?

■ Problem-solve to build new habits. Perhaps you tend to leave your desk cluttered at the end of the day because you're tired and running late. A coach might talk with you about developing a new morning habit of spending ten minutes filing and organizing before you dive into the day's work, or building a habit of filing papers away at various times during the day as you complete a particular task.

Another approach might be to hire support staff to help you maintain your new system.

▌ Provide structure and support as you work to strengthen new habits so that they become integrated into daily life.

Psychotherapists

You may already be seeing a counselor or therapist if you've been diagnosed with ADD. A therapist who is experienced in working with adults with ADD uses many problem-solving strategies that are also used in coaching. However, unlike a coach, who may contact you briefly many times throughout the week, your psychotherapist may see you once a week or less often. Therapy and coaching can often work very effectively hand-in-hand. You may decide upon a new strategy or habit in therapy, and then use your coach to support you with more frequent contacts while you build that habit into your daily routine.

Emotional Issues leading to disorganization

Psychotherapy can also address other sorts of emotional or psychological issues that may get in the way of organization.

Unrealistic self-expectations, for example, may lead you to judge yourself too harshly or set your organizing goals at an unrealistically high level. This is the sort of issue that is best dealt with in therapy.

Depression can be a strong deterrent to improving organization in your life. If you're depressed and tired, the organization of your daily life tends to fall apart. Beds go unmade, bills go unpaid, and laundry goes undone. Without treatment for depression, all the organizing help in the world can't be effective.

Anxiety can drain you of energy and focus, allowing daily tasks to go undone and clutter to pile up around you. The longer you go with unfiled taxes or piles of papers and magazines, the more impossible the task may seem. Even looking at the task can then create waves of anxiety you might seek to escape by escaping the prospect of working on getting organized.

Obsessive-compulsive disorder (OCD), one form that anxiety takes, may cause you to overfocus on tiny details. You may spend hours obsessively reordering your CD collection while much higher-priority items go undone. You may be so perfectionistic that you can't unpack your books because you haven't found the perfect bookcase to put them in. If you struggle with OCD issues you may feel that you are constantly "organizing" without ever getting organized.

A psychotherapist who specializes in treating ADD in adults can also work with you as you learn more about yourself and exactly how you are affected by ADD, as well as to help you develop strategies to counteract these tendencies. For example, if you are very easily distracted from the task at hand, you and your therapist can develop techniques to reduce or eliminate distractions so that you can succeed in completing your organizing task.

Conclusion

The organizing approaches outlined in the rest of this book will suggest approaches that take many aspects of ADD into account, helping you to break down huge projects into doable bits, helping you learn to develop and maintain new organizing habits, providing many levels of external structure and support that will help you get started and keep going. So, start small, get the support you need to keep going, and learn how you can work *with* your ADD to get your life better organized.

Review

■ ADD-friendly organizing strategies can work with structure and support.

■ Organize independently by providing yourself with structure and support.

■ Give yourself permission to ask for help.

■ Ask for help from family and friends.

■ Engage professional organizing help.

■ Decide on the level of support that you need for each organizing task.

Structure and Support

Part *Two*

Taking Charge of ADD

Streamline and Simplify: Counteracting Complications

Karen has been in treatment for ADD for several months. The medication has been helpful, and she's asked for accommodations at work. That has taken the pressure off, but now that the school year has begun again, Karen is feeling overwhelmed. "It feels like I just can't keep up. I ran late today because I couldn't find anything to wear. And I just realized that I am wearing navy pantyhose instead of black! So I'll be running around all day mismatched unless I take even more time out to stop and buy black hose. Why can't I seem to do even the simplest things, like get dressed for work in the morning?"

Karen has two children in elementary school and works full time. In the evening, she rushes home, stops to pick up last-minute groceries, or takeout from a fast-food place, fully aware that she'd rather have a more nutritious meal for her family. She never seems able to work out a menu, shop, and cook. And even when she has shopped for groceries, she may forget to thaw the chicken she's planned for dinner. "I should buy stock in Domino's Pizza!" she jokes.

"And my social life? Ha! Who has time for friends? When would I find the time to clean house, plan a dinner, and invite people over?" She feels out of touch with friends and overwhelmed by the dual demands of work and home.

Simplify, simplify, simplify. This should be the mantra for adults with ADD. Simplification is one of the strongest stress-management and life-management tools that an adult with ADD can learn. The more complex the task, the more chances there are for confusion, forgetfulness, and careless error.

Our busy lifestyles tend to place more demands on us than we can possibly meet.

> ## Is this your story?
>
> ## It is if you:
>
> ▌ feel overwhelmed by home and work;
>
> ▌ find that forgetfulness and lack of planning add to your daily stress;
>
> ▌ feel that daily life is too complicated; and
>
> ▌ can't seem to find time to relax or enjoy life.

Karen, like most women today, is chronically stressed, trying to juggle work and family commitments. Her ADD makes this juggling act even harder because she has greater difficulty developing streamlined routines for herself and her family. In addition, she has difficulty organizing her day, a common problem for adults with ADD. So, on top of an overly busy schedule, she's frequently pinch-hitting. To cut down on stress and the complications of disorganization, Karen needs to find ways to streamline and simplify her life.

Level One Solutions:
Ways to Help Yourself

Simplifying begins with an analysis of the things that trip you up in daily life. Karen's list of daily complications includes:

▌ dressing for work each day;

▌ dressing the kids for school;

▌ preparing breakfast;

▌ packing lunches;

▌ departing with all items necessary for the day's activities;

▌ preparing dinner;

▮ doing laundry; and

▮ finding time for contact with friends.

Whatever you place on your list of daily tasks or routines that frequently go wrong or that frequently cause stress, your next task is to ask yourself how you might streamline or simplify it. Many adults continue with routines that don't work well, never stopping to strategize, to create a simpler approach. Here are some strategies that worked for Karen.

Simplifying Getting Dressed

▮ Develop a color-coordinated wardrobe.

▮ Pare down what's kept in the closet so that clothing can be easily found.

▮ Choose easy-care fabrics that require no ironing.

Organize your wardrobe around one color

Karen has solved her own wardrobe problems by organizing her winter wardrobe around one central color, black. She tops off several black skirts and pants with solid-color blazers and knit tops of black, red, or another color. She has reduced her blouses to only those that coordinate well with the pants, skirts, and blazers. Pantsuits are also an excellent wardrobe choice because all that's needed is a blouse. "I own two black handbags, one for everyday and one that's dressy. My shoes are black, and my hose is either neutral or black (no navy!)."

In the spring and summer, Karen's wardrobe revolves around white and green. There are many shades of green, and when different shades are mixed and matched with a second color or with white, her wardrobe has enough variety to carry her through two seasons. "Simplifying my wardrobe has brought many benefits," says Karen. "I save money on clothes. I save time on shopping. I have more room in my closets. And the anxiety of knowing what to wear is over. I'm so much less overwhelmed."

Shop for clothes with a "closed mind"

Being closed-minded as you shop turns off distractions, limits choices, and reduces confusion. Structure your shopping by setting a clear goal: for example, a pantsuit and new work shoes. Head straight for the department where those items are sold instead of getting distracted by attractive displays and shouting sale signs. Look for your color scheme first, then your size, then see if the price fits your budget. Save open-minded shopping for vacation and special occasions when you have nothing but time and money.

Simplifying Morning Routines for Kids

▌ Keep socks, underwear, T-shirts, and pants in colorful, labeled baskets—clean laundry is more likely to get tossed into baskets than to be folded and put away in drawers.

▌ Only buy matching socks— for example, white athletic socks without stripes.

▌ Keep a second set of toothbrushes in the powder room so kids don't have to go back upstairs to brush after breakfast.

▌ Eliminate distractions such as morning television to keep kids on track.

▌ Have "grab and go" healthy breakfasts on hand for mornings when you're running late.

▌ Prepack lunches.

▌ Create a "launching pad" next to the door to hang jackets, backpacks, sports equipment, and any other items that need to be taken to school (or work).

"We're just an ADD family," laments Karen. No matter how hard we try, we can never get up early in the morning. Instead of continuing to feel guilty about the sweets her kids eat as they ran out the door, Karen rethought the morning meal. "Why don't I just accept that we won't have a sit-down breakfast, and plan something nutritious that the kids can grab and go?"

Nutritious "Grab and Go" Breakfasts

▪ yogurt with fruit on the bottom;

▪ individual containers of two-percent milk or skim chocolate milk;

▪ cheese sticks and crackers;

▪ fruit of any kind;

▪ frozen breakfast sandwiches that can be heated in the microwave;

▪ multigrain muffins;

▪ bagels and jam; or

▪ peanut butter and jelly sandwiches (the kids' suggestion).

Prepacked lunches

The daily lunch dilemma had a remarkably easy solution. Every Sunday night, the kids each prepack five lunch bags with lunch staples, such as cheese sticks, yogurt, a piece of fruit, a baggie of raisins or trail mix, and a nonperishable drink. The lunch bags are stacked in the refrigerator. If there's time, a sandwich can be quickly added in the morning before school. If not, another healthy snack item can be tossed in the bag.

Creating a "launching pad"

A launching pad is a place, conveniently located near the door, where all items are kept that family members need to "launch" into their day. Laundry rooms, mud rooms, or a corner of the kitchen can often serve the purpose. Karen created a launching pad near the kitchen door that led to the garage. Each child has his own colorful plastic crate in which athletic cleats, sports equipment, or sports bags were placed. Two shelves on the wall are labeled—one assigned to each child—to provide a place for musical instruments, art projects, or anything else that needs to be taken to school the next day. On the wall, each child is provided with two hooks—one for his backpack, the other for a jacket or sweatshirt. A third, higher shelf serves as Karen's launching pad. On it she places clothes to take to the dry cleaners, purchased items to return, and anything else she needs for the next day. Her briefcase is placed on the floor, while two wall hooks are used for her coat, umbrella, scarf, and purse.

Reducing Search Time For Key Items

Despite her launching pad, there are certain things that Karen still scrambles to find. For example, she can never seem to find her cell phone when she is ready to leave in the morning. It's a small frustration that just about drives her crazy every day. Now she keeps her cell phone in a bright yellow leather case. It also has a beeper on it. From her kitchen phone, she can press a button that makes her cell phone produce a chirping sound so that she can find it.

Another daily frustration for Karen was her difficulty in quickly finding essential items in her purse. Cleverly, Karen solved this problem by choosing a different bright color for her wallet, change purse, pens, and comb. Before, most of her accessories were black. Now, a quick glance for the right color ends her search. Karen eliminated her searches for keys by purchasing a large metal clip to attach her key ring to her purse strap. The clip allows her to tuck the keys inside her purse, but prevents them from falling into the abyss.

Streamlining Dinner Planning and Preparation

Dinner has always made Karen feel particularly guilty because she often resorts to "fast-food fallback." The solution is a weekday meal rotation (Monday through Thursday). With input from her children, Karen made a list of eight simple meals for her weekday rotation. Simple means no more than two main ingredients.

During Week 1, Karen serves	On Week 2 she serves
▪ spaghetti ▪ grilled cheese and tomato sandwiches ▪ chicken potpie with rice ▪ turkey hot dogs with beans	▪ tuna sandwiches with tomato soup ▪ frozen stir-fry vegetables on rice ▪ macaroni and cheese ▪ hamburgers

With each meal, Karen serves prepackaged salad or fast-frozen vegetables. Fridays are pizza or taco night. Saturdays and Sundays can be take out, cooking on the grill, eating out, leftovers, or a more elaborate sit-down dinner when possible.

The meals repeat every two weeks, but there is enough variety that the kids never tire of them and enough simplicity that Karen (and the kids) find them easy and quick to prepare. Karen's shopping list is standard. "It's so easy to shop, even my husband can do it now!" Karen calculates that the time she saves on simplified meals, plus not wondering about what to serve and what to buy, saves her several hours a month.

Simplified grocery shopping: The supermarket sweep

Make a sweep through your supermarket and see what is in each aisle. Arrange your shopping list roughly parallel to the way your supermarket is organized. Use your list to shop by aisle and you'll shave up to 35 percent off your shopping time.

Buy in quantity. With her eight rotating meals in mind, Karen was soon able to stock up on sales items that fit into her biweekly routine, saving both time and money. The prepacked lunch routine and the "grab and go" breakfast routine also helped structure her grocery shopping and allowed her to buy in bulk.

Simplifying Your Social Life

Although regular entertaining is still out of the question for now, Karen began to look for ways to be in touch with friends on a more regular basis. Now that her dinner preparations are more streamlined, she has developed a regular routine of calling a friend for a chat as she cooks.

Plan low-effort social events

She's become more realistic about what she can squeeze into her busy schedule. But instead of going without social contact altogether, Karen and her husband make regular plans to meet friends at a local restaurant or to catch a movie together on a Saturday night. "It's great. It feels more like the early days, when we had less money, but more fun."

Introduce regular, automatic social gatherings

Now that she understands the important roles that *structure* and *support* play in creating an ADD-friendly life, Karen applies that to her social life as well. She has joined a book club with a friend. This gives her a regular routine that ensures she'll have friendly social interaction on a monthly basis, without having to initiate and schedule it herself. The structure of the book group has an added advantage. Karen is now finding time to read a book each month—an enjoyable activity that she had neglected after the kids were born.

Simplifying Exercise

Every working parent has a right to the stress-releasing and physical benefits of exercise. Parents of ADD children and parents who are themselves ADD need to regard exercise as part of their lifelong plan to cope with ADD. To simplify your exercise routine, choose a program that requires little or no equipment to remember, maintain, store, or purchase. Walking, running, stretching, yoga, swimming, and many other exercises qualify. Another way to simplify exercising is to build it into other aspects of your day—making a routine of taking the stairs at work, or parking a distance from your office and then walking to and from your car each day.

Level Two Solutions:
Help from Friends and Family

Don't Shop Alone

Bring along a friend—or your clutter companion who is less likely to be thrown into confusion if you shop at stores that are not well organized, such as discount or outlet stores. While these stores can save you money, their inventory is not as well organized as at a regular department store. Sizes are jumbled. Styles are mixed. The jumble and confusion of searching for a bargain may cause ADD patterns to intensify to such an extent that you forget what you came for and begin to shop in a reactive or impulsive mode. A clutter companion is a friend or family member you can call upon to help you organize your things, clutter, and possessions because they are good at it themself. Your clutter companion can help you cope with the confusion of outlet store chaos.

Streamlined Exercise with a Friend

Simplified, streamlined exercise is more likely to fit into your busy schedule, but doing that exercise with a friend adds structure and support, so you're likely to exercise more consistently. Look for a time of day that is convenient, and support each other in getting more regular exercise. Many adults find it convenient to take a brisk walk during the lunch hour. While jogging requires a shower and change of clothes, walking requires only comfortable shoes.

Create an ADD-Friendly Closet with the Help of a Clutter Companion

 Many adults with ADD make better and faster wardrobe choices when the choices are easier to see, when there are fewer choices, and when outfits are preassembled. The answer is to create an ADD-friendly closet. A clutter companion or PO can help you organize an ADD-friendly closet. Hang your clothes in your closet by complete outfits. Match a skirt to a blouse or a pair of slacks with a top and jacket. You can even preselect jewelry or accessories; put them in a plastic bag and hang them all together on the same hanger.

Take the clothes out of your dresser drawers, fold them neatly, and stack them on your closet shelves. Or put the clothes in attractive see-through boxes and stack the boxes on the shelf. Retire your dresser.

Keep a large plastic bag in your closet. If you find anything you can give away, put it in the bag. Take the bag to a women's shelter or a thrift store when it's full.

Level Three Solutions: Help from Professionals

Use a Personal Shopper

Better department stores are staffed with personal shoppers. You tell them what you want and your size and they make the selections for you. Then, all you need to do is go to the store, look over the selections, and choose from among them.

Personal shoppers are paid a percentage of the cost of the clothing that you purchase, so be sure to set a clear budget for them. Cut out magazine and catalogue pictures of outfits you like. Hand them over to your personal shopper with your color preferences and sizes and wait for a phone call to see your options.

Other Personal Services

Increasingly, as our lives have become busier, many other personal services have become available, especially in urban areas. If such services are in your budget, you can find companies that will run all sorts of errands, help with common chores, and do other sorts of shopping for you. If such services are not affordable think of creative ways to barter with friends, exchanging errands that are convenient for you to accomplish for other errands that may be more convenient for your friend.

Simplicity Partners

If you are in therapy with an ADD specialist, he or she can serve as a partner for reviewing your daily life and discussing the things that routinely overwhelm you. It may be difficult for you to see ways to simplify and streamline your daily life. ADD coaches and professional organizers are typically very experienced in simplifying and streamlining—not only helping you to streamline daily routines, but also helping you to streamline your environment to support those new routines. You may find that you need professional support in the beginning, as you learn to streamline your life. It's important to develop the habit of streamlining and simplifying all aspects of your daily life. It's a powerful ADD-friendly organizing strategy to build into your life.

Review

▮ Simplify, simplify, simplify.

▮ Simplify your meals, wardrobe, social life, and exercise.

▮ Create a launching pad.

▮ Be a closed-minded consumer.

▮ Set up an ADD closet.

▮ Work with others to simplify and streamline.

Chapter Five

ADD Decision Dilemmas

June looks out her window at the pouring rain and the water gushing from her gutters. She calls several contractors from among the mass of business cards she has acquired. Each contractor provides June with ever more detailed information, and all their quotes are wildly different. "I guess I need more information," June thinks. She is no closer to replacing her gutters now than she was two months ago.

Tommy, June's son, is ten years old and looking forward to going away to camp this summer. It's mid-April, and June's dining room table is overrun with brochures, newspaper clippings, and Internet printouts about summer camps. Selecting a camp has turned into a very time-consuming project. June wants to be sure she makes the best choice possible, but the camps are filling up fast.

Paradoxically, the more June tries to make the perfect decision about every aspect of her life, the more out of control her life feels. Time slips away as time-critical decisions are not made. Deadlines are missed, not due to procrastination, but because her anxious perfectionism prevents her from reaching decisions.

Alicia, another woman with ADD, also struggles with decision-making. The process overwhelms her: the more information she gathers, the more choices she has, the more frustrated and confused she feels. In her attempts to plan a family vacation, for example, the number of possibilities overwhelms her, and a kind of paralysis sets in. Should we go to the beach or the mountains? Should we visit nearby family members, or fly to Florida to see the grandparents? In the end, having made no decisions, she and her husband pile the kids in the van and take off, picking a route almost at random, deciding to "sight-see" along the way. Alicia feels immense relief—the burden of deciding was lifted—but is disappointed in the vacation that results.

> ### Is this your story?
> #### It is if you:
>
> - have difficulty reaching a decision;
>
> - overwhelm yourself with information and details before choosing;
>
> - resort to making an impulsive decision, just to "get it over with"; or
>
> - allow people or circumstances to decide for you.

John's ADD-related decision-making struggles are different. John tries to avoid decisions altogether. He never feels sure of the correct decision, so he prefers to let people and events chart his course. His strategy in life has been passivity. By avoiding decision-making, he believes he can also avoid responsibility for the outcomes of decisions. Not surprisingly, John is married to a take-charge woman—someone who has always made plans for John, and who organizes his life.

Perfectionist Indecision

June's efforts toward perfectionism can be the result of several ADD issues. For some, perfectionism is a way to compensate for the disorganization, distractibility, and impulsivity of ADD. This type of adult with ADD is a "compulsive compensator." The compensations they've developed have become so strongly ingrained that they seem compulsive. For example, one man with ADD became compulsively neat because, when his surroundings are cluttered, things seem to "disappear" all the time. For years, he has arranged his keys, wallet, cell phone, loose change, and even the tie he has just taken off neatly on his night table. To the outsider, this behavior may seem fussy and overly tidy. He has learned from experience that when he lets these carefully developed habits slip, he won't be able to find his car keys or wallet.

For others, perfectionist tendencies may have developed in response to criticism. In some adults, especially in women, persistent negative feedback results in chronic anxiety. For example, June's mother was very controlling and demanding, a former schoolteacher who had stayed home to focus all of her energies on her daughter. June anxiously learned to double- and triple-check herself, expending most of her emotional energy trying to gain her mother's approval. Now, in adulthood, she has internalized her mother's harsh criticism and feels compelled to do everything perfectly.

June's attempts to be perfect come at a very high cost. She expends too much energy on unimportant decisions, and even misses deadlines in her driven approach to gathering every possible bit of information.

Impulsive Decision-Making

Another ADD pattern, impulsivity, can also unduly influence decision-making. Impulsivity is the tendency to act without fully considering the possible consequences; in other words, leaping before you look. For some adults with ADD, decision-making occurs on impulse. They act on emotion instead of reason, and often later regret their actions. For impulsive adults with ADD, decisions can greatly improve by resisting the impulse and taking time to think it through.

For many others, though, what may appear to be impulsivity is actually a reflection of a difficulty with thinking things through and considering the options. Such an adult may think about a decision for a long time, speaking to many people in the process, only to make an impulsive decision in the end, just to "get it over with." In other words, the ADD difficulty with executive functioning—with information gathering, evaluating, considering possible consequences, and ranking the choices—is so difficult for them that they resort to metaphorically flipping a coin or throwing a dart.

Decisions by Default

Others with ADD, like John, deal with their difficulty making decisions by avoiding them altogether. For example, one young man with ADD felt overwhelmed by the college application process. Despite prodding and nagging from his parents and high school guidance counselor, he continued to procrastinate—never writing his college essay or mailing his applications until most deadlines had passed. In the end, he was admitted to a local state school that had a rolling admission policy and no college essay requirement. His college decision was made "by default"—after many opportunities had passed him by as he avoided making choices and acting on them.

Level One Solutions:
Ways to Help Yourself

Solutions to Perfectionist Decision Blocks

If you are a "hunter," always seeking the perfect answer, choice, or solution, your expedition can take you almost anywhere—to the Internet, the library, into many discussions with many people, on a search through magazines, newspapers, and into your own world of needs, wants, preferences, and ideas. This search for the perfect choice is very time consuming. But, if you "fence in" your hunting ground, it will set an objective limit to your hunt, reducing choice and increasing the prospects of succeeding in your hunt for a good decision.

The time limit fence

The search for a perfect summer camp is meaningless if the camp application and payment arrives late. June might first look at the camp application deadlines. They are likely within a week or two of each other. To be conservative, she could choose the earliest deadline from any camp. On her calendar or day planner, June should enter the camp decision deadline as if it were an appointment with herself. Then, because there is so much reading material and Internet research to do, it would be best if she actually blocked time out on her calendar or dayplanner to achieve this.

Butting up against a time limit fence will not ensure that June will make the perfect choice. Truth is, she can only make her best choice. No choice is perfect. But a time limit will ensure that a choice does get made, that it is as well informed as time permits, and, most important, that it is timely. Tommy might not think his summer camp is perfect, but he sure will like it better than missing out on camp altogether. Make the best decision you can given the time you have.

The budget limit fence

Use your budget limit as a fence, and your choices will automatically be reduced. With her budget limit in mind, June is able to discard out of hand many of the gutter repair offers and the summer camp options. June observes, "I am not frivolous financially, but it is easy for me to not pay much attention to my budget when I look at glitzy brochures of summer camps, or alluring pictures of beautiful houses. The fewer choices I have, the better. Once I set a budget limit, it is easier to get past the glitz to the bottom line of cost." Make the best choice, given your budget.

Create a physical limit as your fence

If you tend to be a perfectionist, it is likely that the internal signal that says, "Stop! Enough is enough" may not go off. You need an external signal to compensate for the lack of an internal one. Set up an external physical signal that tells you when to stop when your internal signal does not.

Find a physical container for your choices, options, and possibilities. For instance, a basket for vacation brochures, a cubbyhole for credit card offers, a box of decorating ideas, or the entire surface of the dining room table for summer camp information. When that container is full, you have reached your limit. It does not matter how much new material you come across. The fullness of the physical container is your signal to stop and make a decision.

Create a numerical limit

Decide to obtain three estimates for a household repair. Then go with the best option.

Decision-Making

Dealing with Decision Overwhelm

The impulsive escape from decision overwhelm

It's important for you to distinguish *true* impulsivity from impulsivity as an escape from overwhelm. For those with ADD who are truly impulsive, important decisions may be made on spot, sometimes in the heat of the moment. If impulsivity causes you to leap now and look later, you'll probably need professional help in learning to overcome these patterns, and may possibly need to consider stimulant medication as part of this process. In this instance, however, we are not addressing *true* impulsivity, but the kind of impulsive decision—"what the heck" decisions—that result from frustration with indecision. These impulsive decisions are often a reaction to too many choices. For example, Alicia's impulsive decision to take off on a driving vacation followed months of indecision. She didn't make an impulsive decision off the bat, but only after she'd been unable to reach a considered decision. Too many options were on the table; too many family members disagreed about what should be done.

The passive escape from decision overwhelm

When you let people and events decide for you, you're probably feeling decision overwhelm, but your escape is passivity rather than impulsivity. Most likely, you haven't liked the outcomes of many decisions in life that were made *for* you, but at least you could shrug and tell yourself, "It wasn't *my* choice." But, in fact, the choices *are* yours! They're just not very well controlled choices. When you choose to let circumstances decide, the outcome is more risky.

In certain circumstances, passivity is relatively cost-free. Pizza or Chinese? Go to the movies, or rent a DVD? Perhaps you don't really care and would prefer that your companion do the work of deciding. But what about important decisions? Stay here or move to L.A.? Go to college or get a job? Accept a promotion or keep doing the same old thing? The cost of passivity becomes much higher.

Solutions to overwhelm

When overwhelm leads to either impulsive decisions or passive decisions-by-default, look for ways to reduce overwhelm. Overwhelm can occur when you're overstimulated (for example, in a crowded, loud, or noisy environment), when you have too many choices, or when you're trying to please too many people. The best way to avoid decision overwhelm is to limit the input.

- Shop in smaller stores with fewer displays.
- Limit the number of options to consider before you decide.
- Identify the most important issue (price, convenience, practicality, and so on) and then focus on that factor to make your decision.

Use Your Own Yardstick: Value-Based Decision-Making

Decision-making often feels overwhelming if you're not using your own values as a yardstick. For example, one young woman with ADD was considering the purchase of her first home. She felt completely overwhelmed by the number of factors to consider. Should she move to the outer suburbs, where she could purchase a larger house for the same price? Should she think about resale value, or go with her personal preferences? How much should she be willing to pay for a shorter commute? Everyone gave her differing advice. Instead of enjoying the prospect of owning her own home, she felt stressed and frustrated. Ultimately, she realized that the advice she received from her parents, her realtor, and her friends shouldn't cloud her own values and preferences. Once she trusted her own feelings and reactions, the decision-making process became clearer. "My father kept telling me, 'Look for the least expensive house in an expensive area.' But I didn't really like any of the homes that filled that bill. One weekend, I walked into a house and just *knew* that it felt right—for me."

Supports: Rewarding Yourself

You can support your efforts by rewarding yourself when you have passed a decision-making milestone. Rewards along the way can reduce the frustration of delayed gratification and are essential to keep you going on any long-term project.

| Level Two Solutions: | Honor the |
| Help from Friends and Family | Difference between Small and Large Decisions |

 If you are in doubt about the difference between a small and large decision, consult with your time tutor (or PO, therapist, or ADD coach). From a time management point of view, the preoccupation with the hunt can be a real time waster, especially if the decision is small but the hunt is large. Choosing a summer camp is a bigger decision than choosing Tommy's T-shirts for camp. Don't spend the same amount of time on each. Finding a good gutter contractor is a bigger decision than finding the perfect beige gutter. Keep your hunt appropriate to the size of your decision. Time is precious. Spend it wisely.

Prioritize Decisions and Spread Them out over Time

What is more important, a mother's self-care or caring for her children? Her commitment to the community or needed home repairs? Attending a school meeting or an environmental task force meeting? All of these things are important, but they are not all equally important at the same time. And that is the key. People who manage their time well have a natural instinct for not only the relative importance of things to each other, but for what is important when. But many people try to do all the important things with the same intensity at the same time.

A time tutor can be of great help in putting priorities in order and phasing decisions in over a period of time. "I decided that my health (teeth) and my son's homework come first right now," June decided. She notified the community group that she would finish the project she was currently working on, but could not attend meetings again until Tommy left for summer camp. She let the environmental group know that her child's academic needs were her priority at present. For now, she would send them a larger donation than usual and read their newsletter to keep informed. Spread your important decisions and commitments out over time.

Use a Stop Coach

If you have difficulty knowing when enough is enough, you might want to ask someone without ADD to help you determine when you are finished. For instance, June is writing an article for her church on religion and the Internet. But the article never seems to end. She's missed one deadline already but hopes to make the next one. A church member who writes could tell June when the article is finished, when it has said enough to the reader to inform them but not overwhelm them with everything there is to say on the topic. We call this person a stop coach. Stop coaches can help you end writing and research projects, bring renovating and decorating to a conclusion, and add closure to organizing projects.

Use a Decision Coach

Often, it can be very helpful to talk through a decision with someone who can help you gain a different perspective. Alicia, in struggling to make a vacation decision, was stuck in the ant's perspective—running here and there, looking at details—airline schedules, brochures, input from multiple family members. She never stopped long enough to step back and think about her values and objectives. Alicia jumped from one possibility to the next, never deciding, never clear on her priorities.

Clarify your thoughts with a decision coach

Talking with a decision coach—a friend or family member—can frequently clear the way to making a decision that feels "right." A decision coach is not just one more person who offers you their opinion, but rather someone who can help you clarify your own thoughts and feelings—by asking questions you've been too distracted to ask yourself. A decision coach could have asked Alicia questions such as: What are your goals in choosing a vacation? Do you want to expose your children to new experiences to broaden their horizons? Or does you family need a relaxing vacation, with time to reconnect, while doing low-stress, familiar things? Or is connecting with far-flung family members at the top of your list? Had Alicia been asked these questions, and thought about them, she would probably have made a more satisfying choice than the ill-planned road trip that was the eventual result of her indecision.

Decision-Making

Turn Black-and-White Decisions Into Gray Ones

Working with a decision coach can help you to think things through. Again, the role of a decision coach is not to give his or her own opinion, but to help you think things through and break things down. Some choices are all or nothing, once in a lifetime. We grab at the brass ring or we don't, and that's the end of it. But most choices are not that black and white, although they may seem so to you.

A decision coach can help you think of ways to turn a black-and-white choice into shades of gray. For example, you may have been offered a job opportunity in a distant location. Although this may be presented as a "yes or no" decision, perhaps it need not necessarily be so.

Explore options with a decision coach

A decision coach can help you explore options you're not aware of. Is there a possibility of a temporary assignment? Is there a possibility of returning if the job doesn't work out? How about visiting the area for a number of days to gather information? What is the possibility of postponing reassignment until your oldest child graduates from high school next year? Do I negate future opportunities if I turn down this one?

Even if you decide against this opportunity, talking your decision over with a decision coach may open up new ideas for you. For example, this opportunity may make you more aware of the value of advanced training. Perhaps you'll decline this offer, but decide to return to school for more training to increase your chances for future offers that are a better fit for you or your family.

Level Three Solutions: Help from Professionals

Decision-making and Reaching Goals

Many decisions are necessary in order to meet a goal. You must:

- decide upon an appropriate, realistic goal;
- decide upon an ADD-friendly plan for reaching your goal;
- decide upon the steps required;

▪ decide upon the level of structure you need to succeed in your goal; and

▪ decide upon the supports you'll need to keep your motivation high.

Your PO or ADD coach can help you make decisions at each step—from goal selection to goal completion—keeping the three S's—strategies, structure, and support—in mind.

Structure: Setting Milestones

Milestones provide structure in the course of a long-term effort. Your PO or coach can help you establish milestones (to measure and mark your progress).

ADD-Friendly Strategies

Your PO or coach can help you set goals and use strategies to reach those goals that work *with* your ADD.

Right-brain approaches for right-brain people

Many adults with ADD are right-brain thinkers. Everyone uses both sides of the brain simultaneously, but each hemisphere serves different functions. The left brain is oriented to traditional organizing strengths like sequencing, ordering, and analysis. But if you are right-brain dominant you'll tend to be a visualizer, and more intuitive instead of a goal-oriented planner. Dr. Lynn Weiss writes of right-brain tendencies among her clients with ADD:

> Cesario . . . "goes with the flow" . . . often effectively using feelings as a guide. To Cesario, the journey tends to be more important than the goal. It is not that he doesn't have or reach goals . . . it is just that he reaches them in his own way, frequently creating an experience in the process. (p. 35)

Let the goal choose you

Dr. Jane Petrick, the director of Informed Decisions International, advises, "We are most effective, not when we choose the goals, but when we let the goals choose us." Letting goals choose you is a very right-brained process. However, planning, by its nature, is left-brained, using logic and sequence. If you are right-brained, a completely left-brained planning process is unlikely to work well because it does not use your creativity or access to your intuitions. When a plan doesn't "feel right" to you, it's not likely to work. It's critical that you find a PO or coach who understands your right-brained approach to the world, and who can help you develop strategies that are compatible with your style.

Give up getting it right

"In the common daily life most of us lead, 'getting it right' is a cultural obsession," notes Dr. Fred Newman in his book *Let's Develop!*

> "Our culture is a culture of getting. Perfectionism is taken as a sign of how good we are as getters. This preoccupation with right-ness is a fanaticism . . . and it produces one of the quintessential postmodern diseases: stress." (p. 170)

A better philosophy than "getting it right" is doing your best. If you have given something your all, that is the best you can do. Even the best information is filtered through our imperfect desires, wants, and preferences. There is no perfect outcome, only the best effort.

After many struggles, June finally reached this conclusion. "I realized that no matter which of the final two camps I decided to choose, Tommy was going to have a great time. And if for some reason he turned out to be unhappy, we'd deal with that when it happened." June had spent her life anxiously gripping the wheel, trying to avoid every pothole in life. Finally, she realized that she could cope with the bumps if they occurred. June was working on another essential executive function—shifting actions as needed when circumstances change.

When Psychotherapy May Be Necessary

If you find that decision-making fills you with dread or anxiety, you may need to see a therapist. Also, you might not be the best judge of how injurious your brand of perfectionism, or your need to be right, is. You might not cause yourself emotional pain, but if you see that it distresses others, like your spouse or coworkers, it might be wise to consult with a therapist, if only to hear an objective opinion.

Review

▮ Set time, budget, and physical fences to limit perfectionist hunting.

▮ Reduce decision overwhelm.

▮ Use your own yardstick to make value-based decisions.

▮ Honor the difference between small and large decisions.

▮ Prioritize decisions and spread them out over time.

▮ Use a stop coach.

▮ Use a decision coach.

▮ Turn black-and-white decisions into gray ones.

▮ Set decision-making milestones to structure the process.

▮ Reward yourself, and seek supportive encouragement from others.

▮ Consider setting right-brain goals.

▮ Give up getting it right.

▮ Consider psychotherapy if decision-making causes you great anxiety or dread.

Decision-Making

B-o-r-i-n-g:
Managing Stimulation Hunger and Hyperfocus

Jerry is a very bright but bored certified public accountant. He struggled with ADD issues throughout high school and college, switching from a science major to accounting after a "crash-and-burn" freshman year at college. Jerry's ADD and basic lack of interest in accounting have resulted in a checkered career path. At age thirty he is on his third job. "Even if a job interests me, after a short while I feel bored and want to move on. I just can't seem to settle into anything," Jerry says.

Because he gets such little gratification from his job, Jerry is engaged in all kinds of activities at night to compensate for his boring days. He belongs to an investment club, plays cards regularly, and gets lost for hours in computer games. He also loves late-night TV and rarely gets enough sleep before his alarm rings in the morning. Jerry's mornings look like a juggling act. He checks his e-mail in the morning and cannot resist responding to some of it as he gulps down cereal standing up. He takes a quick look at his online investments as he heads for the shower. Dressing is always complicated by shirts not pressed well enough and jackets with missing buttons.

Jerry watches TV as he dresses, catching the morning news and traffic report. As he gazes at the TV, Jerry is unaware of time slipping away. He is so captivated that if he never had to go to the bathroom he might still be standing there! He glances at his watch, realizes he's running late, grabs his briefcase, scrambles for his cell phone, and searches for his keys. His chronic lateness is affecting his performance reviews at work, and he's in danger of losing his job.

Marge doesn't seem to resemble Jerry on the surface. Although they both have ADD, Marge goes through her life at a much slower pace. Unmarried, Marge lives alone and works as a paralegal in a downtown law office. Marge is very bright. Attorneys in the firm sometimes joke with her that she can do legal work better than they can. The truth is, Marge *is* as bright as the attorneys, but a spotty academic record and lack of role models precluded her from gaining acceptance to law school. Often she feels frustrated and bored by her paralegal work, but with little else going on in her life she works long hours, sometimes on weekends when a big case is pending. She is able to focus and organize at work, but her personal life is a different story. Her apartment is extremely cluttered and rarely cleaned. She is hyperfocused on work. Neglected friendships have faded away. Her only regular social contact is attending church on Sundays.

> ## Is this your story?
> ### It is if you:
>
> - cannot tolerate boredom;
> - crave stimulation;
> - tend to develop addictive patterns of stimulation seeking;
> - let "escape" activities interfere with responsibilities; and
> - tend to hyperfocus and lose track of time.

Stimulation Craving and ADD

Many people with ADD crave stimulation. In fact, some researchers hypothesize that some ADDers have a "risk-taking gene." Although we don't really understand the neurological mechanism, the ADD need for stimulation is well known. It is more obvious among hyperactive/impulsive ADDers because their stimulation seeking is quite observable, from fast driving and fast talking to sky-diving. But even quiet, inattentive-type ADDers stimulate themselves through daydreaming, television, escape novels, and over-eating if the events around them aren't interesting. Thom Hartmann, a well-known writer on the topic of ADD, hypothesizes that those with ADD crave a sense of aliveness more intensely than others. Some ADDers are so intolerant of boredom that they start an argument or create a crisis to avoid understimulation. Stimulation-seeking behavior can be either your key to success or your undoing, depending upon how it is managed.

Destructive Stimulation

While Jerry seeks stimulation in a very active, sometimes hyperactive fashion, Marge's stimulation seeking is more passive, but equally destructive. Stimulation for Marge comes in the form of soap operas that she carefully tapes during the day to watch in the evening, and from online shopping, and overeating. Now in her late thirties, Marge's weight has ballooned to over two hundred pounds. No matter how many diets she tries—and she has spent a fortune on them—she has never been successful in maintaining weight loss. Her credit cards are all charged up to the limit and she struggles to make minimum monthly payments on them.

Because Jerry cannot tolerate boredom, he seeks stimulation—from his computer, the newspaper, and television. Even lateness is a stimulant for Jerry. Jerry may not *want* to be late, and he tries not to be, but the short-term effects of the stimulation generated from lateness are undeniably engaging. There is the stepped-up whirl of external commotion. There is the brain engaged in simultaneously remembering where things are, processing information from the computer and TV, internally creating an excuse for being late, and so on. Things may be chaotic, but they certainly are not boring! However, lateness is a destructive source of stimulation with numerous negative effects.

Level One Solutions:	*Reduce Stimulation-*
Ways to Help Yourself	*Seeking Distractions to Manage Lateness*

As Jerry engages in multiple activities during his morning routine, he predictably loses track of time. A "minute" checking his e-mail becomes fifteen. A quick glance at the newspaper stretches out, then something on the television news catches his ear and he's glued to the TV, listening to exciting news of the latest disaster. With a morning routine that is so stimulating and distracting, it's no wonder he's usually late.

The solution? Limit the distractions. Only the threat of being fired motivated Jerry to go "cold turkey" with his morning distractions. On the advice of his therapist, he decided to keep the door to his bedroom shut in the morning, a big reminder not to enter and check his e-mail. He cancelled his subscription to the morning paper as well. His new morning routine is to get up, shower, dress as quickly as possible, and leave for work immediately. With an earlier departure, he arrives at his office building way *ahead* of schedule. He can purchase a muffin, newspaper, and cup of coffee in the deli on the ground floor, and be at his desk, enjoying his breakfast and morning paper, when his surprised but very pleased manager arrives a few minutes later.

Look for Constructive Sources of Stimulation

One of the driving forces behind Marge's compulsive overeating patterns was stimulation hunger. Women with ADD who crave stimulation often satisfy their craving in passive ways—television, shopping, eating, and substance abuse.

Instead of focusing on trying to eat less, Marge began to pay attention to her need for stimulation. Because initiating and scheduling are typically difficult for those with ADD, Marge sought groups and activities that met at regular, scheduled times. First, Marge joined a singles discussion group at her church that met on Sunday evenings. A few weeks later, an ad caught her eye for a master's program in business management that offered evening classes for adults who work full-time. She called for more information and decided to enroll for the fall semester. A notice for yoga classes caught her eye and she signed up for a ten-week class.

Within a few months, Marge's work was no longer the center of her life, and her compulsive overeating patterns began to lessen as her evenings filled with more interesting and stimulating activities.

Manage Hyperfocus

Jerry, like many people with ADD, tends to hyperfocus on activities that are highly engaging. Hyperfocus has to do with the disregulated attentional system of the ADD brain. Most adults with ADD find that they are prone to attention difficulties at both ends of the continuum. In some situations, they are highly distractible; in other situations, they hyperfocus to the point that it is very difficult to shift their attention. One woman with ADD reported that she was so involved in working on writing a paper that she didn't know her building was on fire until firemen burst into her room, amazed to find her at her desk!

When you are hyperfocused on a book, TV program, or favorite activity, you may find that it is very difficult to pull yourself away—to "transition" to another activity—because you are so involved. Often, it requires a strong external signal—an insistent reminder from someone, hunger, fatigue, or a ringing phone—before you can unplug from hyperfocus. For Jerry, hyperfocus on morning distractions caused lateness. At night, hyperfocus on escapist activities prevented him from getting to bed on time.

One pitfall of hyperfocus is losing track of the passage of time. This full engagement creates a kind of outside-of-time experience; time seems to be adrift. When engaging in hyperfocus, you need to arrange for external reminders so that you don't become oblivious to life's other commitments.

Hyperfocus, when it occurs, is involuntary, but typically it's quite predictable. Most likely, you hyperfocus on select activities. Typical hyperfocus activities include:

- working;
- watching television;
- reading;
- playing computer games;
- gambling;
- shopping; and
- surfing the Internet.

Hyperfocusing becomes problematic when it causes lateness because you've lost track of time, or when your difficulty shifting out of hyperfocus leads you to neglect responsibilities and relationships. It's important that you develop ways to snap out of hyperfocus when it's time to turn to other activities.

- Set an alarm clock or use an alarm watch.
- Arrange for a beep (audio or vibrating).
- Program your computer to send you a "Stop" reminder.
- Impose a strict time limit or spending limit.

Using hyperfocus constructively

Like many ADD traits, hyperfocus can become a very positive force in your life if you use it strategically. So don't just think in terms of *controlling* your hyperfocus, but also in terms of taking advantage of it. Some of the most spectacularly successful people are those with the ability to hyperfocus. The key is that they have constructed a life in which they hyperfocus on career-related activities. Do what you love, and you can put your hyperfocus to work.

Many adults hyperfocus only on leisure or escape activities and never think in terms of constructing a career that allows them to focus on their interests. Some interests may not work as a career focus, but if you think creatively about what aspects of your leisure activities draw you into hyperfocus, you'll be surprised at how many career paths involve similar activities.

Level Two Solutions:
Help from Friends and Family

Help from Others in Managing Hyperfocus

You may find that when you're engaged in certain activities, your own efforts to end hyperfocus are not successful. When this happens, you'll need to strategize with others to manage your hyperactivity.

When your hyperfocus is extreme, extreme measures may be necessary. For example, one computer analyst tended to become so hyperfocused on his computer work (using his hyperfocus constructively!) that all of his efforts using alarms and reminders were ineffective. He had missed or arrived late to so many meetings that, finally, he requested that the administrative assistant for his group come to his office door, grab his attention, and remain there until he pulled himself away from his computer to attend the meeting. His wife learned a similar technique, calling him on his cell phone to pull him away from work at the end of the day. Just as with the administrative assistant, his wife's efforts were successful only if she kept his attention by keeping him on the phone as he reported, "I'm standing up, grabbing my briefcase, turning out the light, shutting the door, and heading for the car." Once he'd started his car engine she'd succeeded in her task!

Friends, colleagues, and family members can help manage your hyperfocus in a variety of ways.

- ▌ Ask them to tell you when "time's up."

- ▌ Engage in hyperfocus-type activities with another person. You're more likely to be able to shift from hyperfocus when they shift.

- ▌ Arrange for someone to call you on the phone to snap you out of hyperfocus. Depending upon the strength of your hyperfocus, they may need to keep you engaged in conversation while you "snap out of it."

Don't abuse the structure and support provided by others, however. You need to develop strategies for avoiding hyperfocus at critical times. For example, don't kid yourself and begin a hyperfocus activity half an hour before it's time to go home for the day, or half an hour before bedtime. You may need help with hyperfocus, but you can't completely shift responsibility to others or your support system will begin to fold.

Using Your Time Tutor to Manage Hyperfocus

They don't call it the Web for nothing! The Internet is a place perfectly designed for hyperfocusing. You can get stuck in it like the prey of a spider. Jerry invests online and though his philosophy is to invest for the long-term he feels compelled to check his investments several times a day. There are colorful charts to see, graphs to track, research to conduct, intriguing information, and the opportunity to chat with others.

With the help of his time tutor, Jerry says, "I've put myself on an 'Internet diet.' I restrict myself to one hour online, three days a week, and set an alarm to tell me when my time is up." Computer games are another of Jerry's hyperfocus traps. Instead of playing them alone, he now plays computer games with other people. Now computer games are entertainment, a chance to socialize with friends instead of being purely an escape.

Level Three Solutions:
Help from Professionals

You may find, especially if your stimulation hunger plays a very destructive role in your daily life, that you'll need a higher level of support at first—from an ADD coach, PO, or ADD therapist—to build new habits and to find constructive ways to use your hyperfocus and manage your stimulation hunger.

Use Your Stimulation Hunger for Career Advancement

Jerry's need for stimulation, especially in the morning, had led to problems in meeting daily responsibilities. Even at work, Jerry had frequently resorted to surfing the Internet or playing computer games surreptitiously when he became bored with his routine accounting work. A plan that required Jerry to ignore his stimulation hunger could never have worked for long.

Instead, Jerry and his therapist developed a plan to *use* his stimulation hunger to become more successful in his career. Instead of continuing to do the repetitive, uninteresting accounting and tax work that he found so mind-numbing, Jerry went to his supervisor and expressed an interest in setting up seminars to train other accountants in the firm how to use the very complex new software that the firm had purchased. A computer whiz, Jerry was the ideal choice, and a much less costly choice than hiring outside consultants to do the training. Jerry's ADD-related traits of being very active, both physically and verbally, made him well suited to training others. Finally his interest in computers could be used to his advantage at work, rather than used as an escape from work.

The Cutting It Close Game

In the Cutting It Close game, the PO suggests a strategy that appeals to many hyperactive adults with ADD because it introduces a fun challenge to the task of getting to work on time, making a tedious task much more stimulating.

Being prompt can be very stimulating if you make a game of it. You can play the Cutting It Close game with your PO. To win, you must get to work (or school) exactly on time, not a minute sooner and not a minute later. To play, you and your PO have to construct routines that ensure perfect promptness.

In Jerry's case, to achieve perfect promptness he needed not only an evening routine that jumpstarts his morning, but a morning routine that gets him to work exactly on time (occasional lateness for events beyond one's control are permitted). So with his PO Jerry took a close look at his morning routine and put together a plan to get to work right on the button.

"It took me eight days of tinkering with my routines to win at Cutting It Close. But I can't tell you how much more fun it is to make a game of getting to work right on time without a minute to spare. Yesterday, I beat my personal best and got to work early!" exclaims Jerry.

Review

- Seek constructive sources of stimulation.
- Avoid counteracting boredom with risky or escapist behaviors.
- Develop strategies to transition from hyperfocus.
- Learn techniques to limit hyperfocus escapes.
- Recognize how hyperfocus affects your time awareness.
- Play the Cutting It Close game.
- Seek a career that feeds your stimulation hunger.
- Put your hyperfocus to work *for* you.

Chapter Seven

First Things First:
Learning to Prioritize

"**A**nyone who looked at my life from the outside would think I have it pretty good," Jim remarked. "I've got a good job, a great family, and, thanks to my wife, our household runs pretty well." But suddenly, after a recent medical checkup, Jim was looking at the high price he'd silently paid to keep up his daily pace. "Keep going like this," his doctor had warned, "and you may be heading for an early heart attack."

Jim's childhood hyperactivity had transformed into mental hyperactivity as an adult. He was a great problem-solver and trouble-shooter in his job, and juggled his demanding schedule by frequently staying up well beyond bedtime to catch up on bill paying, tax returns, or other work. Jim joked that it was a good thing he was hyperactive, because otherwise he'd never get everything done. Jim hit the ground running each morning. "I'm out the door early to beat the traffic. No matter what I'm doing all day, it feels as if I ought to be doing something else—when I'm in the car with the kids, I'm talking on my cell phone to my boss. If I'm out of town on a business trip, I feel bad that I'm missing the kids' soccer games."

I'm Running as Fast as I Can

While Jim raced through his days at top speed, like many adults, real exercise was sorely missing from his busy life. His weight had been creeping up. "What exactly am I supposed to give up to fit in exercise? And how am I supposed to find time to eat healthy meals when I can barely manage to grab a fast-food lunch during the day at work? And what about when I travel?"

Is this your story? It is if you:

- live in crisis mode, reacting to the demands of circumstance;

- tend to "squeeze it in" rather than eliminate items from a crowded agenda;

- think that everything belongs on your "A" list of daily to-dos;

- rarely step back to consider what "really matters"; and

- let others set your priorities for you.

Too Busy to Prioritize

Instead of planning and prioritizing, Jim had always coped with overload by working at warp speed, neglecting his personal health and giving up much-needed sleep whenever he was in a crunch. His doctor insisted that he make regular exercise and good nutrition a priority. "Prioritize?" Jim asked. "How do you do that? It's *all* important! I've got a job to do, kids to raise, a house to maintain, a wife, a family." Now, for the first time, his old ways of coping couldn't work. In fact, they were a big part of the problem. Instead of racing and juggling, he needed to learn to prioritize—not so easy, and even more of a struggle when you have ADD.

The Challenge of Prioritizing

It is only when we take stock that we can prioritize, asking ourselves, "Is this really necessary?" "If I'm going to take this on, what am I going to give up?" "Am I really living my life according to my deepest values, or just reacting to whatever pops up?"

Prioritizing is difficult for everyone, especially in the fast-paced life that so many adults live today, bombarded with choices and burdened with high-pressure jobs in addition to the responsibilities of home and family. When ADD is added to the mix, prioritizing often goes out the window in favor of rapid reaction—reacting to demands as they hit you, without deciding whether they are your top priority. Rarely, in a jam-packed day, does an adult with ADD take time to realistically assess what can be accomplished and then prioritize, asking, "If I can only accomplish three tasks on my list, which three should I choose?" Often, top-priority items may be the least likely to be chosen, while many less important things are placed first.

Poor prioritizing patterns

Instead of prioritizing "first things first," many people make choices according to other rules:

- **Whatever's on top.** Paper shuffling.

- **Whatever's the easiest.** Easy does it.

- **Knock-knock.** Responding to whomever asks me first.

- **False progress.** The more I can check off my list the more productive I feel.

- **Proximity**. Might as well do it while I'm passing by.

- **You decide.** I don't want the responsibility.

- **Conflict avoidance.** If you yell loudly about something, it'll go to the top of my list.

- **Whatever I'm in the mood for.** I'll do it if I feel like it.

- **Save the worst for last.** Anything but that!

- **Go with the flow.** Doing whatever the others do.

- **Habit.** Just doing the usual.

All of these ways of "prioritizing" aren't really prioritizing at all. In fact, they are ways to avoid prioritizing, letting habit, circumstance, or the priorities of others determine how you spend your time. Adults with ADD who "prioritize" according to these rules often find that they've never met many of their life's goals.

They're All on My A List!

At the other end of the prioritizing continuum are those with ADD who put *everything* on their A list. Instead of passively letting people or circumstances decide their priorities for them, they frantically try to take charge of their lives.

Anne was an A List prioritizer. She had so many top priorities that they all interfered with one another. Her aging mother had recently moved to the area to be near Anne. "I want to spend time with my mother. Who knows how many good years she has left." Anne's son and daughter were both in high school. She tried hard to be at all of their sports events and to work with them nightly on homework. Exercise and nutrition were high on Anne's list. She had a running partner and worked hard to fit in a morning run on weekdays. Anne had a background as an urban planner, and currently was engaged in contract work with a local urban planning consultation group. The demands of her work varied, but could be quite intense at times. Anne's marriage was another top priority. The marriage had become increasingly strained as both she and her husband were overcommitted and chronically stressed. They had entered couples counseling to improve their communication patterns and to work on making their marriage a priority in their busy lives. Anne's efforts to reduce stress and to get in touch with what's really important in life had led her to join a women's spirituality group at her church—a group that met weekly.

The harder Anne tried to make everyone and everything in her life a top priority, the less she succeeded. Unable to set priorities and set limits, the end result was that everyone in her life felt short-changed while Anne raced in frantic circles, never sure what commitments should take precedence. The A List approach to prioritizing leads to failure because if *everything* is important, then nothing is treated with importance.

Level One Solutions: Ways to Help Yourself

Take Time for Daily Quiet Reflection

When the pressure is on, ADD impulsivity often leads people to dive in and work as fast as they can instead of stepping back to look at the big picture. Instead of prioritizing, you're just putting out fires. Instead of hitting the ground running, as Jim described his mornings, try a different approach. Get up fifteen minutes early, make yourself a cup of coffee or tea, and go to a quiet place in your home to think and prioritize.

Think about your day, not just in terms of the actions you must take immediately, but also in terms of your long-term goals. Set the day's priorities accordingly.

Slow the Flood to a Trickle

Too often, today, we are bombarded from all sides—by choices, by opportunities, by responsibilities, and by information. Consciously choose to limit your exposure to this bombardment from advertisers, newspapers, radios, televisions, and magazines. Mark out time on your calendar to do "nothing." The fewer choices and the fewer demands upon us, the easier it becomes to prioritize.

Rotate your Priorities

Adults with ADD often have a broad range of interests, and often attempt to pack too many of those interests and activities into each day. Instead of giving up an interest, think instead of "rotating" them. For example, Joan developed better focus and balance in her life by rotating her activities according to the season. In winter months, Joan focused on indoor activities—reading, cooking, and playing the piano. She attended more cultural events during the cold months, enjoying season tickets at a local theater and attending movies or concerts. In the spring, she rotated her priorities to gardening and bike riding. In the heat of the summer months, she spent her leisure time traveling or relaxing on her deck. Then, as cooler weather came in the fall, she returned to more active pursuits. Her friends often asked her how she could "do it all"—cooking, reading, attending cultural events, gardening, playing the piano, riding her bike, and traveling to exotic destinations. Her secret? She didn't do it *all at once.*

The Neglected Four

Time-management experts find that, of all high-priority activities, four are most neglected: socializing, doing paperwork, reading, and exercising. These activities are neglected because they place no clear, active demand on us for our attention and time. In a packed schedule, you are more likely to respond to things that *must* be done today, or things that call your attention: dinner must be served, children demand your attention. Meanwhile, your paperwork, book, and treadmill sit quietly by, and friends who don't keep calling you go neglected. Ultimately, you pay a high price for this neglect.

Socializing

You're more likely to stay in touch with friends if you can see them at regularly scheduled events that don't require planning and initiation on your part. Clubs, book groups, support groups, and school activities all fit the bill. Another approach is to set aside a regular monthly time and write it in your calendar—for example, schedule a lunch date for at least one Saturday per month.

Doing paperwork

Paperwork should be regularly scheduled into your plan for the week. By scheduling a weekly time, you can pay bills the first and third weeks of the month, leaving the second and fourth weeks for filing, balancing your checkbook, completing forms, and making phone calls related to paperwork issues. If it is difficult for you to do paperwork for an hour at a time, break it up into smaller chunks. Some people prefer to "process" their mail and paperwork on a daily basis—spending fifteen or twenty minutes a day instead of an hour or two weekly.

→ Plan your paperwork slot for a time when you're not fatigued.

Keep paperwork in a clear plastic container, place it in your briefcase, and process it on your lunch break if you're too fatigued to do paperwork in the evening. Or, set aside a couple of hours on the weekend.

Reading

To read more, make it easier to read and more difficult to watch television, or whatever other activity interferes with reading. For example, remove the TV from your bedroom. You'll be more likely to read when you get into bed at night. Schedule regular times for reading professional journals, newsletters, and other materials necessary to keep you up-to-date (and to control your stacks). Always keep reading material with you so that any waiting time can become reading time.

Exercising

We all need proper exercise to meet the demands of everyday life. It reduces stress, increases mental clarity, and generally keeps us fit. Regular exercise is a critical part of ADD management, helping to reduce stress and feelings of restlessness. Regular exercise is difficult to maintain— but it's more likely to happen if it's part of your daily pattern plan. Build in exercise patterns with a friend and you'll find that it happens more often. Walking is the simplest form of exercise to build into your day. Bring your lunch and walk during lunch, eat outdoors, and walk back to work. Take the stairs. Get a dog, and you'll automatically need to walk twice a day!

Socializing, doing paperwork, reading, and exercising are appointments you make with yourself. Don't give them up without a fight! If a friend calls and your schedule says "paperwork" fight for your time to do paperwork. Tell your friend you are unavailable and put them in the socializing slot, or, better yet, invite your friend to do paperwork with you at the library or local coffee shop. Giving up your paperwork slot should be your last resort.

Level Two Solutions:
Help from Friends and Family

Support Groups

Anne was on the right track when she joined the women's support group at her church. On some level, despite her overcommitted schedule, she was aware that she needed to get back in touch with the things that matter most in life. A support group can provide you with *structure* through its regularity, and can provide you with *support* from group members as you work to achieve more balance in your life.

Examine Your Priorities with a Trusted Friend or Family Member

When you feel stuck, unable to prioritize, conflicted by your commitments, you may gain a better perspective by talking things out with a trusted friend or family member. Karl had always made community involvement a high priority in his life, serving on the local PTO, coaching his children's sports teams, and serving on the board of his community organization. As his family grew, he and his wife decided to remodel and expand their home rather than move out of the community where they had developed such strong roots. As the remodeling plan was under way, however, Karl's stress levels rose and he felt that his priorities were increasingly conflicted.

After several conversations with his wife, his priorities became clearer. A larger, more comfortable home would significantly improve the quality of life that he and his family would enjoy. The children would have a recreation room of their own, a place where they could enjoy socializing with friends. He and his wife would have a quiet refuge in a new master bedroom suite. But, for the moment, his commitments to the community organization and the PTO would have to take a lower priority so that the remodeling project could move to the top.

Help with the Neglected Four

A time tutor can help you develop a daily plan that includes time for these neglected four. Instead of waiting to *find* time for them, you and your time tutor can *make* time for them by placing them in your week's schedule.

 Your time tutor can help you identify patterns in your day that waste valuable time that would be much better spent on the neglected four.

Level Three Solutions: Help from Professionals

Get in Touch with Basic Values

If you're like Anne, daily moments for quiet reflection may not help you set priorities. You have too many A-list priorities to comfortably fit all of them into any one day. When this is the case, you may need to gain perspective by talking with a therapist, taking a look at unrealistic expectations of yourself (and others' expectations of you) and your inability to set priorities. Anne, like the "old woman who lived in a shoe," had so many priorities she didn't know what to do.

A therapist can help you better understand what drives you in your efforts to be all things to all people, or to be accomplished at all things. Setting priorities cannot mean saying "yes" to everything. By its very nature, prioritizing is a process of deciding what is more important than other things in your life, a process of achieving balance in your life.

Prioritizing with a PO or ADD Coach

A PO or ADD coach can help you assess the practicalities of your priorities. By assisting you in making more realistic time assessments and creating workable plans for your day, your priorities will be more likely to fall into place. A coach or PO can help you stay in touch with doing "first things first," instead of simply reacting to whatever life throws at you during the day.

Review

▪ Don't let people and events prioritize for you.

▪ Not everything can be on your A list.

▪ Take time for daily reflection.

▪ Learn to make time, don't wait to "find" time.

▪ Slow the flood to a trickle.

▪ Rotate your priorities.

▪ Gain perspective through explorations with others.

▪ Work with a therapist to examine basic values and unrealistic expectations.

▪ Work with a PO or ADD coach to stay focused on doing "first things first."

Chapter Eight

Out of Sight, Out of Mind (OosOom):
Remembering to Remember

On Edgar's couch is perched a slightly precarious stack of empty picture frames. "I plan to go to the do-it-yourself frame store soon and spend the day there framing my posters and photographs," Edgar explains. The chair near the front door holds several shopping bags. "I've got to return those to the store." Edgar's dining room table serves as his household finance center, complete with heaps of bills to pay, piles of investment material to review, and bunches of bank statements to reconcile. Out in full view is a lamp to rewire, a chair to recane, and a weeder to unsnarl. Short stacks of books and videos line the floor beneath his bay window. "I have to remember to return those to the library," he explains. Boxes of greeting cards for every occasion, along with gifts to wrap and decorations to put away, take up half the kitchen table.

Out of Sight, Out of Mind

Like many adults with ADD, Edgar is an "OosOom"—an out of sight out of mind person. Edgar does what he can see, and does not do what he cannot see. So if Edgar wants to be certain that the books get returned to the library and that the greetings cards go out on time, he must have them out in front of him. The things to return to the stores, the framing project, and even bill-paying chores must be in full view as daily visual reminders of tasks to perform. Without his things as prompts and cues, Edgar would simply not remember to do what he needs to do.

> ## Is this your story?
> ### It is if you:
>
> ■ have a home cluttered with "reminders";
>
> ■ tend to be forgetful; and
>
> ■ have difficulty remembering to do future tasks.

Edgar does not prefer that his home look this way. He'd rather put the broken things out of sight and the papers in files so that he can entertain his friends in comfort and style. But he's afraid, and rightly so, that he'll simply forget to pay his bills or fix his lamp if the visual cues are gone. "The thought of putting things in the closet or storage shed fills me with fear," he admits.

Why Are So Many People with ADD OosOoms?

Many people with ADD have a problem with "prospective memory"—memory for tasks that must be completed at a future point in time. They are OosOoms—out of sight is out of mind—without a visual reminder of what they need to do, they often forget.

If you have ADD, you may have an excellent memory in some respects—for example, you may have an uncanny knack for remembering random facts—but a poor memory for daily tasks, such as returning videos or library books. Returning a library book may seem simple, but, it can be much more challenging than recalling facts. To remember to return a library book, you need to keep that "to-do" in mind and pull it up at exactly the right time—just before you pass the library. If you recall it too soon, you may forget it again. If your recall it too late, you've already passed the library. In fact, chances are, you may not remember it until you see the library book on the back seat of your car the next morning. "Oh no! I forgot *again*."

Remembering to Remember

Forgetting Due to Hyperfocus and Distractibility

While hyperfocus can bring great energy to the task at hand, your prospective memory pays a price. Your attention is entirely focused on what you *are* doing, leaving no attention to remembering intended future actions. For others with ADD, distractibility, rather than hyperfocus, is the culprit. When you are bombarded by immediate distractions—a phone call, a shop window, a chance encounter with a friend—you may be prone to forget an intended task. Tasks that must be completed in a specific sequence (on your way home from work) or at a specific time (call home at 4 P.M.), are most vulnerable to forgetting because the window of time during which we must remember them is very small. Other prospective memory tasks are more forgiving. If you forget to water your plants or to put the laundry in the dryer, you can do it later today, even tomorrow, with little ill effect.

Level One Solutions:
Ways to Help Yourself   *Contain Yourself!*

Most adults with ADD need some type of "cue" to remember to perform the task. Auditory reminders such as recorded messages can help, as can written to-do lists, but the best cue is a visual cue. A visual cue is a permanent cue that continues to remind you as long as we see it. Keeping everything in sight in stacks and piles is a form of visual cueing. The problem is that such visual cueing can lead to clutter and chaos.

Instead of cluttering your environment with visual cues, contain yourself with visual cues. When you view your things, it directly "tickles" your memory to take action. The trick is to make things visible and visually appealing at the same time. Open baskets, clear shoeboxes, acrylic bins, see-through plastic drawers, even large plastic food storage bags are great in-sight in-mind tools. Put everything you possibly can in clear containers that reveal the contents but are attractive to look at.

How to Shop for Organizing Containers

Containing yourself is fun and easy, but shopping for containers—well, that's a different story. The number of choices and the stimulating variety of colors and shapes can be overwhelming to anyone. It's easy to buy too many containers or ones that don't really do the job because the stores they go into are filled with so many choices. Unfortunately, buying one of each is often the result. That just clutters up your home with containers!

Take these steps:

▍ Measure what you need before you go. Draw little boxes on paper and jot down the dimensions.

▍ Bring along Polaroid pictures of the clutter you want to contain or the space where you want to put a container.

▍ Go to a good-sized store that has several departments so you can find what you need all in one store.

Vision Drawer Tower

Clear Snap Case

Courtesy of the Container Store.

Skylight Storage Container

Courtesy of Rubbermaid
Home Products.

Courtesy of Rubbermaid
Home Products.

Remembering to Remember

- Think plastic, then wood, then wicker, then metal. Hit the home décor, storage, or closet department first. Try kitchen and bath departments next. Home office, stationary, and hardware departments can also be great sources of containers. Don't worry about the name of the department you are in. You can find great container solutions for kitchen things right in the bathroom department.

- Shop with a friend. It will keep you better focused.

Create a "Take Me with You" Basket

Next to Edgar's daily exit door is placed a large, open, flat woven basket. It looks great. Inside are things that need to go to and from the house to the car and destinations beyond. Film to develop, store returns, and stuff to go to Edgar's office are in the basket. He just scoops the stuff up on his way out the door.

Create an Errand Box

The clutter of things in your home often represents incomplete tasks and projects that you do not want to forget to complete. Much of this clutter is actually in transition to the car.

Your errand box is an open plastic crate on the *front* seat of your car that contains all of the visual reminders for the day's errands. Move your items from the take-me-with-you basket to your errand box as you move from house to car.

For instance, if you're an OosOom and you toss a book to return to the library in the back seat of your car, you can easily forget about it. But if you toss the library book in your errand box on the front seat, you'll have a clear visual reminder to go to the library. This errand box has the added advantage of having the books handy right in the car with you when your prospective memory kicks in and you suddenly remember to go to the library; obviously, you don't want the clutter of your house to simply migrate to your car. A full errand box is your cue to run errands.

Make Stubby To-Do Lists—An ADD-Friendly Reminder Habit

A to-do list is another visual reminder. If you find that to-do lists haven't worked well for you in the past, try developing the daily habit of making a "stubby to-do list." A stubby to-do list is bold and big and hard to ignore. It is also very short, with no more than five items on it. Too often, people make long, unwieldy to-do lists in their planner, or worse yet, on a slip of paper they stuff in their pocket or purse. On a long list, items become lost in the shuffle and lose their sense of priority.

How to make a stubby to-do list

1. Purchase brightly colored sticky notes—that are lined and large enough to write five to-do items in large print using a felt-tip pen.

2. Write no more than five to-do items on the paper in lettering about ½ inch high.

3. Write only to-do items that you intend to do *today.*

4. Choose a single place to keep this list—try sticking it to an item that you keep with you at all times—like your purse, briefcase, or Palm Pilot.

5. Make a new stubby to-do list each evening. Keep the felt-tip pen and sticky note pad in a convenient place so that you can add items during the evening as you think of them.

6. Transfer any undone items from today's list onto tomorrow's, but keep it to a maximum of five items.

7. If you find that most days you transfer items over to tomorrow's list—that's a clear indication that your list is too long.

8. Set a goal of shortening your list until it's realistic to complete it on most days.

Remembering to Remember

Edgar's stubby to-do list looks like this:

- ☐ *Buy* basket for front door

- ☐ *Return* library books

- ☐ *Pay* bills today!

- ☐ *Return* video

- ☐ *Send* birthday card to Mary

Your stubby to-do list will be most effective if you write your to-do's in order. For example, if Edgar plans to mail the card in the morning, that should be moved to the top of his list. If bill paying takes place at home in the evening, it should go last on the list.

> **➤ Start each item on your to-do list
> with a verb—an *action* to get you going.**

Develop Habits

Habits, by definition, are a memory enhancement tool because when something is habitual it requires less of our memory. A habit is something we do almost without thought. A bus driver, for example, is extremely unlikely to drive past a bus stop, because he has a very ingrained habit of stopping there. You, on the other hand, forget to stop at the video store because it's not a daily habit.

You may protest, "I've never developed a habit in my life!" Whether you're aware of it or not, you have many daily habits—the habit of hitting your snooze alarm several times before getting up, for example, or the habit of tossing your coat on the chair instead of hanging it in the closet. You develop these habits because they're easy; they're compatible with immediate needs.

In developing new habits, try to use the same concept. Habits will develop more easily if they are designed to be most compatible with your body clock and with your lifestyle. For example, if you are typically very tired in the evening, try to develop a bill-paying habit that takes this into account. Pay your bills in the morning, on the first and third Saturdays of each month. Or you might develop the habit of taking your bills to work to pay during your lunch hour twice a month. Place your bills in a clear folder, put them in your take-me-with-you basket, and then grab them on the way to the office. (See Chapter 2 for more on ADD-friendly habit development.)

Daily, weekly, and monthly habits are useful and reduce the forgetful factor in life maintenance.

Daily habits might include:

▌ a morning routine

▌ a routine for daily errands

▌ a meal-preparation and clean-up routine

▌ a routine to prepare for the following day

▌ a bedtime routine

Weekly habits might include:

▌ a laundry routine

▌ a routine for watering houseplants

▌ a house-cleaning routine

▌ a food-shopping routine

▌ car maintenance

▌ a routine to process paperwork

Monthly habits might include:

▌ bill paying (monthly or bimonthly)

▌ changing the furnace filter

▌ balancing the checkbook

Reduce the Stress Level in Your Life

ADD symptoms, particularly forgetfulness, tend to increase in direct proportion to your stress level. In fact, some adults with ADD have learned to use their frequency of forgetting as a quick and easy sign of too much stress. Misplacing your keys, forgetting your doctor's appointment, rushing from here to there, forgetting to bring what you need—these patterns all intensify with stress. The good news is, these same ADD patterns can be *reduced* by lowering your stress level. Some stressors are outside your control, but often ADD stress is self-induced, the result of trying to cram too many commitments into too little time.

Slow down the pace of your day, subtract commitments and complications, and you may be surprised at how much more you remember.

Level Two Solutions:	*ADD-Friendly*
Help from Friends and Family	*Family Reminders*

Families in which one or more members have ADD function best with family structure and support. Group activities are much easier to remember than solo activities. For example, if the whole family is working to develop a better morning or evening routine, then family members can remind one another to stay on track.

Likewise, weekly and monthly routines can become family routines. Bill paying may go more smoothly if you and your partner work on bill paying together at a designated time every two weeks. That same time can become a time for routine discussions of budgets and spending priorities.

Develop the stubby to-do list habit as a family. For example, each family member could have a different brightly colored sticky note pad, all kept in the same place, somewhere very visible and hard to miss—a bulletin board on the front of the refrigerator, or on the table next to the kitchen phone. That way, family members can also write on each other's lists. For example, if your son needs you to purchase something for him the next day, he can write that on your list.

In recognition of ADD forgetfulness, create a family motto:

> **If you haven't written it down,
> you haven't told me!**

That trains all family members to operate in a more ADD-friendly way, a way that helps all of you to remember.

Create Organizing Occasions

Edgar's home is cluttered because he leaves reminders for himself all over the house. The broken lamp reminds him to make the repair. The picture frames remind him to do framing. And so on. But if Edgar had an *automatic* way to remember to take action, he would not need to clutter his environment with *things* to jog his memory. One way to automatically deal with your chores and tasks and actions is to create organizing occasions.

When you create organizing occasions, the occasion— and not the visible stack or pile or clutter—is the reminder. This method is simple, but since it involves marrying thing organizing to time organizing, you'd better use your time tutor to help you. Here's how organizing occasions work:

1. Get your calendar or day planner.

2. Now, walk around your house with your time tutor.

3. When you come upon a stack of clutter, open the calendar to the nearest holiday or other occasion, and assign a specific task to that day.

For example, Edgar and Jeff, his time tutor, came upon his dining room table heaped with tax-related papers. The next holiday or occasion on his calendar was Valentine's Day, so Valentine's Day was designated "tax day" on Edgar's calendar. They next came upon a huge stack of photographs, slides, cameras, and film. Edgar renamed President's Day "photo day" and assigned himself the organizing chore of going through his photographs. St. Patrick's Day was designated as "framing day"—the day on which Edgar would take the prints and photographs he'd collected and purchase frames for them.

Jeff was especially good at finding just the right occasion to convert into an organizing occasion. "Father's Day is not a good time to organize tax papers, since the filing date for taxes will have passed. On Memorial Day all the stores are open, so it's a great day to bring things in for repair. On President's Day the stores are closed—a perfect time to go through photographs," Jeff explains.

Edgar comments, "I like organizing occasions because I don't have to rely on my memory to remember what chore I am doing when. It's all written on the calendar. I put all my stuff away because I don't need it out anymore to remind me. I'm bound to forget on President's Day where I stowed my box of photographs to organize, so I also added that information to the calendar. What a relief to have it all out of sight—but in mind!"

Level Three Solutions: Help from Professionals

The Home-as-Memory Method

You'll need to use a professional organizer to help you with this method because, though easy to implement, it involves physically moving your things around, out of their usual location, which you might find disorienting if you have ADD. And it requires someone with good thing- and time-management skills.

The idea is to turn your entire home into a big memory bank. When you use the home-as-memory method, time is associated with the physical proximity of space. The things you need to remember soonest in time are put in the rooms of the house closest to the front door. The things you need to remember in the long term are put in the rear of the house. As the date for doing something with your long-term things approaches, you move the thing closer in to the front of the house.

Let's say the room closest to your front door is the living room. All items that you need to take action on go in the take-me-with-you basket near the living room door. For *really* critical items, such as a birthday gift to be delivered tomorrow, you might place the gift in the errand box on the front seat of your automobile.

A back room can serve as your long-term memory. If it is only May but you don't want to forget to mail Christmas cards, put them in the long-term memory room. Move them to the short-term memory room as Christmas nears. Projects that have no particular deadline, like picture framing, or the makings of your scrapbook, are better dealt with by assigning them an "organizing occasion." Start them out in your long-term memory room, moving them to your short-term memory room shortly before their assigned organizing occasion date.

More Serious Memory Difficulties

The memory aids discussed in this chapter are appropriate for standard ADD-related forgetfulness. However, there are other factors that may contribute to memory problems. If you are a female in your forties or older who experiences an increase in memory difficulties, you may want to discuss with your doctor the possibility that lowered estrogen levels have added to memory difficulties. If memory difficulties suddenly increase, or become progressively worse, it's important to discuss such changes with your physician.

Identify Ways to Reduce Stress and Decrease Forgetfulness

If you've tried to reduce stress on your own, with limited success, it may be time to work with a professional who can help you do a comprehensive analysis of the stressors in your life, and work with you to find creative strategies for stress reduction. Many adults with ADD become so accustomed to high stress that they are blind to the ADD patterns that contribute to daily stress.

Review

- Acknowledge your out of sight, out of mind (OosOom) tendency.

- Contain yourself creatively.

- Make a take-me-with-you and an errand box.

- Make a stubby to-do list.

- Create organizing occasions.

- Put a time tutor on your organizing team.

- Try the home-as-memory method.

- Work with a therapist or coach to reduce stress.

Part *Three*

Thing Organizing

Getting over Overwhelm

Jane's house has a double personality. In the front rooms of the house, where guests and friends visit, it is neat and well organized. But the rear rooms of the house, which nobody sees, are cluttered with things—all kinds of things. "I love to entertain and have people stay over, but I abandoned that idea years ago when the guest bedroom became a catchall for the overflow from my own bedroom," said Jane. The dresser in the guest bedroom is covered with perfume bottles, unmatched earrings, pens, small batteries, little ceramic figurines, and the ubiquitous loose change. The night tables overflow with magazines, tissue boxes, tape dispensers, and more loose change. The bed itself, though made up, is strewn with clothes. Clumps of shoes and handbags sit on the floor, together with an array of shopping and gift bags, some containing items to return to the store. Pictures to be framed are crowded under the bed. The closets are crammed and the dresser drawers overstuffed.

More than once, Jane has come to the door of this guest bedroom and opened it widely with a determined gusto intending to organize the room. She sucks in her breath, gathers her courage, and takes a step in. Feeling anxious, first in the stomach, and then in the head, a small panic races across Jane's mind as she struggles to find a place to begin. "Where should I start?" she asks herself. For a few moments Jane does nothing at all. Finally, she picks up a handbag from the floor, and then, feeling overwhelmed and ineffectual, she doubts herself and thinks, "Maybe I should begin over there instead."

Jane walks toward her bed, the handbag still dangling from her hand. Halfway on her journey across the room, she spies a tennis racket propped against the wall. Abandoning the handbag, Jane lifts the tennis racket and gives it a good swing. Still holding the racket, she turns slightly and the closet catches her eye. Jane approaches the closet and peers inside. As quickly as she has approached, she walks away, deciding it is a lost cause. Jane looks at her watch. It has been almost half an hour and she's accomplished nothing. She stands and surveys the cluttered room, racket still in hand.

> **Is this your story?**
> **It is if you:**
>
> ■ feel overwhelmed by your disordered environment and don't know where or how to get started;
>
> ■ tend to see the "big picture" rather than details; and
>
> ■ become easily discouraged when you try to organize your clutter.

"I can't get started. The barrage of clutter is too much for me. No matter how hard I grit my teeth and say 'today is the day,' I move from one thing to another, accomplishing very little." Feeling dismayed and defeated, she closes the door in self-defense against too-much-stuff-all-at-once. Maybe tomorrow she'll get it organized. Jane is stuck in "overwhelm."

Overwhelm and ADD

Jane's source of overwhelm is her cluttered environment. However, feeling overwhelmed can be triggered by other problems as well—for example, by having too many commitments and too little time to meet them; by a huge project with a looming deadline; or by having to juggle multiple tasks while being interrupted frequently. Adults with ADD often get stuck in "overwhelm" when the challenge facing them feels impossible to meet. This chapter will focus on dealing with overwhelming clutter, but many of the approaches that we suggest will also work for other kinds of overwhelming tasks.

The path that leads to overwhelm

Clutter tends to accumulate, unnoticed, around an adult with ADD as he or she moves from one act to the next throughout the days—leaving the bedroom without hanging up clothing, leaving the kitchen without putting away the newspaper or placing breakfast dishes in the dishwasher, leaving papers on the desk rather than filing them. Clutter consists of the remains of incomplete tasks. One of the most common "incomplete tasks" in the lives of adults with ADD involves the acquisition of objects—objects that enter the home environment, but are never given a "home" of their own. Individuals with ADD tend to bring things into their environment on a daily basis—mail, newspapers, groceries, other purchases—never taking the time to find an appropriate place to keep them, and rarely taking the time to discard those items that are "just passing through."

As clutter accumulates, overwhelm follows. And feelings of overwhelm often lead to avoidance. An adult with ADD may fall into a pattern of staying away from home, watching TV, or plugging into the computer in order to block out the growing sense of overwhelm. A vicious cycle is created in which overwhelming clutter leads to avoidance and neglect, which only increase feelings of overwhelm.

ADD challenges that get in the way

Organizing clutter is difficult for individuals with ADD. One difficulty lies in staying focused on the organizing activity rather than reacting to more immediate, more engaging stimuli—a letter or photograph, long forgotten, now rediscovered in the effort to organize a shelf or closet, or a ringing telephone. The ADD brain is wired to react—to impulses, moods, people, or events. To be able to remain focused on organizing, an adult with ADD needs to develop strategies to maintain their focus, such as "sprinting to the finish line," using a body double, or turning it into a challenging game (all ADD-friendly strategies introduced in Chapter 2). Another ADD challenge that makes it difficult to organize clutter is difficulty with decision-making—should I keep it or pass it? If I keep it, where should I put it? (See Chapter 5 on decision dilemmas.)

Learn to Maintain the "Right" Level of Focus

It's important, but challenging, to maintain the "right" level of focus while engaged in an organizing task. Adults with ADD can tell many tales of taking the "ant's view" (micro-focus), concentrating on a single organizing or cleaning activity while the rest of their world is falling apart. Often this micro-focusing results from a need to reduce feelings of overwhelm. Jane can manage to focus on one particular item, but when she looks at the whole mess she feels overwhelmed.

One woman, whose initial goal was simply to clean the bathroom as part of general housecleaning, found herself on her hands and knees, scrubbing and bleaching the grout on her tiled bathroom floor. As laundry went undone and dishes remained unwashed, she intensely micro-focused on the tile grout. Needless to say, this wasn't the most productive use of her time, or the highest-priority item on her chore list.

Others with ADD are comfortable only with the big-picture approach to organizing—a macro-focus. Big-picture people with ADD might say, "It's obvious that we need to clean this place up, get rid of half the stuff in the house and clear out the garage." They can see the big picture, but when it's time to get started, when specific decisions must be made, they feel lost. "Where do I begin? How do I decide what to keep, what to throw away? Should I start in the garage or the kitchen?"

Different Levels of Focus Are Appropriate for Different Problems or Goals

Macro-focus

In macro-focus, a focus on the big picture, the greatest effect is achieved in the shortest time. A super macro-focus might mean simply stuffing misplaced items from each room into large garbage bags, labeling them "living room," "family room," or "kitchen," for later reference, and dragging these bags to the garage. If you've got company coming in an hour, you need a super macro-focus.

Slightly more in-depth, but still focused on the big picture, you might go around the house, gathering misplaced items in a laundry basket. Then, like a clerk reshelving items in a grocery store, you return those items to the room, shelf, or drawer in which they belong. You might choose to have a box in each room where you can place items that belong in that room, but don't yet have a "home."

Detail focus

In detail focus, you would work on a single room, or even a single area within a room. Detail focus involves placing every item within that area where it belongs, creating "homes" for items that don't yet have a designated place. Your goal, in detail focus, is "a place for everything, and everything in its place." This detail focus also involves gathering items in separate containers for "reshelving" in other parts of the house, as well as for throw-away, give-away, and long-term storage. At the detail-focus level sorting, and organizing is happening. This level of focus is appropriate once you've gotten your home to a "livable" level in macro-focus. For these detail-focus activities, you are more likely to need the support of a family member or professional organizer.

Micro-focus

This kind of focus is super-detailed and rarely appropriate. An antiques restorer works in micro-focus, carefully cleaning, repairing, and refinishing a valuable piece of furniture. An archivist works in micro-focus, reading each document in detail to determine its value and where it should be filed.

You need to take care that you don't leap into micro-focus as an escape from feelings of overwhelm in reaction to your cluttered environment. In micro-focus, you may escape into the Internet, browsing websites that advertise storage units, shelving, or varieties of file folders, telling yourself that you are being productive. Meanwhile, the items to store, file, or discard go untended. In micro-focus, you might start detailing your car when your task for the afternoon was to clear out the garage. In micro-focus, you might obsessively clean out the metal runner of a sliding glass door with a toothpick, while ignoring the mountain of dirty dishes in the sink.

Flexible focus

The most useful mode is a flexible focus, where you can move from macro to detail focus, and back again, depending upon what is most appropriate.

Level One Solutions: Ways to Help Yourself

If you're like Jane, stuck in over-whelm, unable to get started on an organizing task, following are some ways that you can help yourself.

Think about the Level of Focus Appropriate for the Task

One of Jane's tasks is to organize the guest room closet. Unlike one of the common areas of the house, it's unlikely that there are items in the closet that belong in other rooms, so a macro-focus—gathering and "reshelving" items—won't help. Her task is a detail-focus task—sorting items into throw-away, give-away, and long-term storage containers, then making sure there's a "home" for each item that remains in the closet.

Develop the Habit of Breaking Things Down

Breaking things down means quite literally dicing up an organizing project into smaller parts. For example, instead of tackling an entire closet or room, divide it into parts, such as a dresser, a bed, one side of the room, or a closet shelf. Breaking a task down into parts adds *structure* to your task—one of those three ADD-friendly S's *(structure, support, and strategies)* that can help you to succeed.

Once the whole is broken up into smaller parts visually, it's easier to find a starting point physically. Concentrating on one part at a time and breaking things down counteracts the overwhelmed feelings experienced by so many people with ADD when they face a complex task. And it makes task initiation easier.

Breaking things down exercise

Walk around your home. Open a closet. Notice the parts—shelves, a floor, and perhaps a rod for hanging clothes. You can organize a whole closet one shelf at a time, or do the things on the floor first and then the shelves. Now look at your desk—made up of a desktop and probably a few drawers. You can organize your desk by starting with only one part—the desktop, or even one drawer. Train yourself to see the parts that make up a whole.

Spy Glass

Use a spy glass

Jane first needed to see the parts of the whole in order to break things down. For that she used a "spy glass," a cardboard tube from a paper towel roll, to narrow her visual field. Jane put the spy glass to her eye and scanned the room. Using her spy glass, she could see only one segment of the room at a time, helping her break down her task into parts. She "spied" her dresser and decided to start there.

ADD-Friendly Strategy: Reduce Distractions to Maintain Focus

Sheet sheathes

Then, Jane used another ADD-friendly technique—reducing visual distractions—in order to stay focused on her task. To eliminate distractions due to clutter in other areas of the room, Jane spread sheets over the bed and night tables, leaving only her dresser exposed. Focused only on the dresser, Jane set to work organizing it. Her efforts went well, but not perfectly. Two perfume bottles were discarded outright, but others were kept. Orphaned earrings had to be saved "just in case" the mate showed up, but most of the other jewelry was put back in the jewelry box. The loose change was rounded up and stashed in a nice pottery jar that remained on the dresser top. Pens, batteries, and other small objects were swooshed into the top drawer of the dresser. Once her dresser top was organized, Jane removed the sheets covering her night tables and focused on them.

"I suppose someone more organized would separate out the pens from the batteries and put each in a proper place," Jane remarked, "but this is the best I can do." The important thing is that Jane finished the task to her satisfaction, using ADD-friendly organizing approaches to help her succeed, breaking tasks down—in this case using the spy glass technique, and reducing visual distractions by using sheets to cover distracting clutter.

Get into an Organizing Mood

Jane was able to get in the mood to organize her dresser, but later, her motivation wilted. Jane, like other adults with ADD, has energy and motivation when she is "in the mood." When she's not in the mood, however, sorting and decluttering seems tedious and endless, and she is rarely successful in completing her task.

If you are like most adults with ADD, trying to force yourself to organize through guilt and self-criticism is rarely successful. Instead of barraging yourself with negative messages—"I'm a slob . . . I should be ashamed of myself"—you'll be more successful if you try a more positive, ADD-friendly approach. What are some ways to get yourself in the mood to organize?

Catch the wave

Adults with ADD often get in the mood at unexpected times. You may find yourself sorting through stacks of loose CDs, looking for the cover to a favorite CD, and suddenly find yourself sorting through your entire collection, putting CDs into cases, and cases back into the CD rack. Go with the flow, unless the consequences are negative—for example, don't let the impulse to order your CD collection make you late for an appointment or late to bed.

Get the most bang for your buck

Start with a task that will maximize your sense of progress. When your first impulse is to run and hide, instead, choose an organizing task that will encourage you. Select the most noticeable area that will take the least time. You might even start with the macro-focus technique of sweeping clutter into garbage bags, just to get started. Then, with your main living areas less cluttered, you'll feel more encouraged to take on detail-focus tasks later.

Share the pain

One online ADD support group helped each other complete "odious tasks" by "meeting" online—declaring a goal—immediately tackling the "odious task," and then getting back online to joke, commiserate, and congratulate each other.

Make it more fun

Play loud music that will energize you. Take "dance breaks" to keep your motivation up. Make it a group task. "I'll help you, if you'll help me." Group activities are usually more motivating than solitary ones.

Set up an immediate reward

Plan a fun activity that you'll do as soon as you finish your "odious task."

Be a "one-minute wonder"

Anyone can do most anything for one minute. When you find that you're feeling overwhelmed, dive in, literally, and see what you can accomplish in one minute. Perhaps you could take all the dirty dishes and cups to the sink from the family room. Or, you might gather magazines strewn across the coffee table and floor into one neat stack. Next time you walk into the room, do your "one minute wonder" routine again. Soon, you'll see the chaos receding. As you feel less overwhelmed, you may find that one minute can extend to five or ten before you get that "run and hide" feeling.

"Age" Your Clutter until It's "Ripe"

If reducing clutter is difficult because you're afraid to throw things away that you'll later regret, try "aging" your throw-aways. Sort your clutter into four categories:

1. keep,

2. toss,

3. donate, and

4. age until ripe.

Throw away the obvious clutter. Donate or give away items that are useful, but that you clearly don't want. When you're not sure what to do, place the item in your "age until ripe" container. It's a little like not tossing leftovers from your refrigerator until they're spoiled. Six months to one year later, during your next round of decluttering, return to the "aging" box or bag. It will probably be a much easier decision at that point to toss or donate items you haven't seen or used in months.

Level Two Solutions:
Help from Friends and Family

Work with a Clutter Companion

After Jane organized her dresser, she arranged an organizing day with Peggy, her friend who lives next door. Jane often babysits for Peggy's two children. In return, Peggy periodically comes over to serve as clutter companion for Jane when she's feeling overwhelmed. Their decluttering routine has become a regular event, a couple of times a year, typically just before relatives are scheduled to visit.

How to Work with a Clutter Companion

A clutter companion is much more than just an extra pair of hands. A clutter companion provides structure that helps you maintain focus and support through companionship and encouragement. With a clutter companion by your side, taking a break won't stretch into procrastination and avoidance. However, unless your clutter companion is a fellow ADDer, it's important to explain your needs. Telling her, for example, "It's better if you don't interrupt me when I'm in the middle of a task." Or, "Remind me to take a break in half an hour. Usually, I just keep going until I'm exhausted, and end up leaving a huge pile in the middle of the floor." Or, "Don't let me hang on to everything. I really need to clear out the things I don't wear any more."

Tackling the job

Armed with empty trash bags, cold soda, and an oldies station on the radio, Jane and Peggy tackle organizing the rest of the guest room. Peggy is helpful, nonjudgmental, and doesn't try to force her own methods on Jane. She's an ideal clutter companion.

Keeping it going

Jane gathered clean clothes strewn about the room and placed them on hangers in the closet, while Peggy plucked handbags, shoes, and other nonclothes, gathering them in a big stack. She waited for Jane to finish hanging up clothes so that she would not distract her. Then Peggy held up one shoe, handbag, or belt at a time and Jane announced, "Out," "Donate," or "Closet." When Peggy noticed that Jane was keeping most things in the "closet" pile, she reminded Jane of her packrat tendencies, asking, "Do you *really* need to hang on to this? I haven't seen you wear it in years!" Jane appreciated the reminder, and humorously added a few more items to the "donate" pile.

Maintaining the right level of focus

Working with Peggy helped Jane to maintain a flexible focus. Peggy asked questions such as, "Shouldn't you just get these piles off the floor [macro-focus] rather than cleaning out your old purses [micro-focus]?" Or, "Instead of rearranging the guest room furniture [macro-focus], didn't you want to get this closet organized [detail focus] first?"

Reaching the end

Peggy tossed the "outs" and "donates" into separate plastic bags and Jane put the closet articles away. If something belonged in another room, Jane threw it next to the guest room door for pick-up and delivery to other rooms. Jane did not stop to deliver the items right away. Her juices were really flowing and her energy practically wiped Peggy out.

After clearing off the bed, they cleared the night tables, and then the floor, using the same process—dividing articles into "out," "donate," and "closet." Exhausted, but satisfied with what they'd accomplished, they toasted their success with cold sodas and called it a day.

"I knew that once I got started, I'd get a lot done!" Jane exclaimed.

Level Three Solutions: Help from Professionals

Working with a Professional Organizer

Getting over overwhelm is difficult. If you do not have a trusted friend as a clutter companion, organize with a professional organizer. A professional organizer knows that getting started is a big hurdle for people who feel overwhelmed. A professional organizer can recommend a place to get started, and their hands-on assistance can get you over the initial hump. Working with a professional organizer also mitigates against your feeling overwhelmed by all the detail that is involved in getting organized. You'll take it one step at a time, at your own pace, until the job is done.

When Your Disorganization Goes beyond ADD

In addition to ADD, there are many other conditions that can cause difficulties in daily life management and organization. If you feel paralyzed and unable to act, even with assistance from coaches and organizers, this may be a symptom of chronic depression or anxiety that must be treated before you can take action. If your packrat tendencies are extreme—for example, if you:

▪ find yourself irrationally attached to items, retrieving them from the trash after they've been discarded;

▪ tend to collect huge numbers of items that you can never realistically use;

▪ have accumulated piles of unread newspapers and magazines to the point that it's difficult to walk about;

- feel tremendous anxiety when you try to organize and declutter; or

- feel so demoralized that you are paralyzed by your clutter,

then issues other than ADD may be part of the picture, and may need psychological treatment before you can begin to organize your environment.

Review

- Use the level of focus (macro, detail, and micro) appropriate to the task.

- Break things down visually.

- Break things down physically.

- Reduce visual distractions.

- Get into an organizing mood:

    - Catch the wave.

    - Share the pain.

    - Make it fun.

    - Reward yourself.

    - Be a one-minute wonder.

- Age your clutter until it's "ripe."

- Work with a clutter companion.

- Work with a professional organizer.

- Consult a therapist when it's more than ADD.

Chapter Ten

CHAOS

In many chapters of this book, therapy or counseling is suggested only when other organizing approaches are not successful. In some cases however, treatment for ADD needs to come first, before organizing approaches can be used constructively. This was true in Marge's case.

Marge laughingly describes herself as suffering from CHAOS (the Can't Have Anyone Over Syndrome). Jane's clutter, described in Chapter 8, was confined to the back rooms of her house, and could be described as "contained chaos"—pockets of chaos within a home that was otherwise in reasonable order. In Marge's case, there is nothing contained about her CHAOS. Every room is cluttered with shoes, articles of clothing, piles of newspapers and magazines, as well as plates and cups. Marge describes her second bedroom as a "private landfill." Her dining room table has not seen the light of day since the last time her parents visited from Florida. Even then, her apartment was so chaotic that she "straightened up," with the help of her sister, by stuffing clutter into large garbage bags that were hauled to the bedroom at the last minute.

Routine cleaning in Marge's apartment is next to impossible

because dusting and vacuuming require that the floor and other horizontal surfaces not be covered by clutter. Unopened mail is lost, resulting in unpaid bills, a poor credit rating, and late payment fees she can ill afford. At times, her phone or a utility is cut off, requiring her to take time from work to pay her overdue bill with a cashier's check so that service can be resumed.

> ## Is this your story?
>
> ### It is if you:
>
> ■ feel that most aspects of your life are out of control;
>
> ■ feel too depleted to take care of life-management tasks;
>
> ■ engage in escapist activities (telephone, TV, Internet, shopping, reading) to avoid facing the chaos of your personal life; and
>
> ■ have felt chronically overwhelmed by the responsibilities of adult life.

Marge's chaos is too great to tackle alone, but before she can benefit from the services of a professional organizer, she needs to examine the pervasive patterns that create the chaos in her life. A friend suggested to Marge that she might have ADD. Although resistant to the idea at first, Marge read the book her friend loaned her and recognizes many ADD patterns in herself.

Marge scheduled a consultation with a psychologist who specializes in treating adults with ADD. After an extensive interview about her work history, school history, and family history, she was given a series of cognitive tests. As the psychologist reviewed her history and test results and explained that many patterns she demonstrates are typical for adults with ADD, Marge begins to understand the basis for some of her lifelong struggles. Forgetfulness, poor time management, disorgan-ization, impulsive decision-making, poor sleep habits, and patterns of moodiness and anxiety have been present for years. Although very bright, Marge never earned grades in high school or college that were commensurate with her intelligence. Now, in her thirties, she has achieved some success in her career, but has always had difficulties on the job—trouble with arriving on time in the morning, meeting deadlines, and keeping up with paperwork.

Marge begins treatment for ADD—a combination of psychostimulant medication and regular weekly therapy sessions focus on helping her to understand and take charge of her ADD. She reviews patterns in her daily life with her therapist and discusses different strategies that might reduce or eliminate some of her daily struggles.

The Daily Cycle of ADD Disorganization

A chronic "night owl," Marge often stays up until 2 A.M. or later. In the morning, she hits the snooze button on her alarm repeatedly until she finally drags herself out of bed, arriving late every morning to work. Marge has fallen into a pattern of working late to compensate for her late arrival, not coming home until 8 P.M. or later. By that time, she is in no mood to wash dishes, do laundry, or pay bills. Ignoring the clutter, she falls onto the couch, microwaves a snack for dinner, and eats while watching television. Her evening progresses with phone calls, time spent on the Internet, and watching late-night TV. Finally Marge crawls into bed, reading until her eyelids begin to close in the early morning hours.

Because she rises late each morning and manages her time poorly, Marge always feels tired and in a rush. She rarely takes the time to wash the dishes. Mail goes unopened for days, often buried in piles of newspapers and magazines. Tasks are rushed and rarely completed, adding to the general disorder. The more chaotic her life becomes, the less she can deal with it. Her attitude becomes, "What's one more dirty dish or coffee cup? It will never be noticed in all the rest of the clutter."

Her therapist helps her prioritize the issues she needs to tackle. Once she knows where to begin, her feelings of being overwhelmed lessen. Marge begins to address these issues one at a time. Whenever the "overwhelm" returns, she and her therapist return to her priority list. "First things first. One step at a time" become her mantra.

Increase Sleep to Reduce Chaos

Top priority is given to her chronic night-owl patterns that make it next to impossible to get up on time in the morning. Marge learns that ADD patterns become worse with sleep deprivation. Both ADD and sleep deprivation have a negative effect on the brain's frontal lobes, the part of the brain responsible for judgment, planning, and organization. When an individual with ADD has chronic sleep deprivation, life is almost guaranteed to spin out of control.

Though resistant at first, Marge begins to shift her sleep patterns, gradually working toward getting into bed by 11 P.M., then reading until she feels sleepy. As she falls asleep earlier, rising in the morning becomes easier. Her supervisor and coworkers are pleased and surprised as she begins to arrive at work on time, ready to begin the day.

Seasonal Affective Disorder

During the fall, as the days become shorter, Marge again begins to have more difficulty getting out of bed in the morning. Her therapist discusses the importance of light in regulating sleep patterns and mood. Many women with ADD also have another condition known as seasonal affective disorder (SAD) that causes them to have difficulty rising in the morning, to feel lethargic and depressed, and to overeat during the dark months of the year. SAD can often be treated very effectively by exposure to bright light in the morning. On her therapist's advice, Marge purchases an "artificial dawn" device that slowly brightens her bedroom every morning so that she wakes to a "sunny" day. To her surprise, she finds it much easier to rise in the morning, feeling more alert and energetic. In addition, the use of a high-intensity "light box" as she gets ready for work also increases her energy and alertness.

Building Routines to Reduce Chaos

Once her sleep patterns are better regulated, Marge has more time and energy to devote to organizing other aspects of her life. She leaves work at 5:30 P.M., arriving home with the energy and motivation to prepare a simple, healthy evening meal. With her therapist's help, she develops routines for laundry, bill paying, and washing the dishes. Even with nightly chores to complete, Marge finds she had time to relax, be in touch with friends, and still get to bed at a reasonable hour.

Marge has been successful in developing daily routines that work, but her apartment is still cluttered, and her closets are precariously stuffed with belongings, and the only way she can straighten the living room when someone comes over is to throw everything into the bedroom and shut the door.

Shifting Focus—From ADD Management to Organizing Strategies

With more control of her daily life, Marge feels ready to tackle the clutter. Marge's therapist suggests that she contact a professional organizer to help her rather than trying to take on this huge task alone. The professional organizer talks with Marge at length about the patterns that led to the clutter and chaos of her living space.

Keeping Things in View as Reminders

Part of Marge's clutter is due to her pattern of keeping things in view as visual reminders. The clutter of things around you is one way to cope with ADD forgetfulness. Keeping clothes in view on a chair will help you remember that you want to give them away. Put them in the closet, out of view, and the reminder is gone, and likely the action won't happen. And when procrastination comes into play, the reminder effect may fade. This is true for Marge. As time goes by, the items she leaves in view are less and less effective as reminders and simply add to the clutter of her environment.

The Clutter of Half-Completed Tasks

A major contributor to Marge's clutter is created by activities that are not followed through to conclusion. For example, Marge might start to open her mail, opening envelopes, perusing ads, examining bills—only to leave the pile of opened mail on her table. Half-read books and magazines are strewn across her coffee table. Laundry is dried, then dumped in a chair for sorting and folding that is never completed.

A Place for Everything, and Nothing in Its Place

Marge often arrives home feeling tired, hungry, and impatient, eager for the comfort of lounging on the couch in casual clothes, relaxing while eating a snack. Her coat, purse, and keys are typically tossed on a chair or table. In the bedroom, work clothes are tossed on a chair rather than hung in the closet. Back in the living room, shoes are kicked off under the coffee table, while her plate, eating utensils, and glass are typically left on the coffee table where she eats while watching TV.

Marge's professional organizer has experience with adults with ADD. She knows that Marge can never declutter everything at one time. What Marge needs is a plan—for conquering the accumulated clutter, and for stopping clutter from this day forward. The latter part of the plan requires a few simple routines to curtail clutter creation at its source. Marge, now on medication and able to concentrate like never before, is a great student. With the PO's support and encouragement, Marge puts in place the routines for household cleaning, laundry, the dishes, and the mail that she and her therapist helped create.

Conquering the backlog requires that one take different approaches. The help of a professional organizer and an assistant—together with Marge's hard work—will be necessary. Marge, better rested and more able to take control of her time because of the support of therapy, is now eager to take this hard work on.

Level One Solutions: Ways to Help Yourself

Routines for Laundry and Household Cleaning

There is a rhythm to laundry, and once you learn the rhythm it goes pretty quickly. Have two laundry baskets, a dark one for dark clothes and a white one for whites. Load the dark items first into the washer. Once the load begins (don't forget detergent!) you'll have thirty to forty minutes before a second load goes into the washer and the first goes to the dryer. Set a timer with an alarm if the alarm on the washer is not loud enough to catch your attention. Set your alarm again when you put that load in the dryer, and place your "whites" in the washer. That way your clothes won't sit in the dryer and get wrinkled requiring a lot of ironing—something you definitely want to avoid. You'll have about thirty to forty minutes each time you load either the washer or the dryer. When the drying is finished, which usually takes another thirty to forty minutes, fold the dark clothes and pop your whites into the dryer. You have a final thirty to forty minutes to wait for the last load.

Altogether, on laundry day, you'll have three thirty- to forty-minute segments available for other activities. Use them to conquer handwashing laundry or household chores that won't take you far afield. Don't run errands, visit with friends, or get into a computer project that requires deep concentration during the thirty- to forty-minute slots. You'll never get back to the laundry. Instead, use your laundry minutes to do time-limited chores such as:

▌ hang up your clothes;

▌ put clothes away in the dresser;

▌ gather clothes together to go to the cleaners;

▌ rinse out hand laundry;

▌ strip the beds;

▌ match socks and put the orphans aside until next laundry day, when their mates will magically appear; or

▌ organize the linen closet (but not the clothes closet—that's much too distracting and too big a job to do on laundry day).

Depending on your family size, your need to do laundry will vary. But count on roughly two hours once a week. If you're fortunate enough to be able to afford it, many cleaning services will also do the laundry for just a few dollars more.

Routines for General Housecleaning

A great system (another word for "routine") for household cleaning for people with ADD (and those without) is the "Mount Vernon method," based on the way George Washington's estate in Mount Vernon is cleaned. For people like Marge, it's ideal because it follows a routine, but has enough variety to keep you interested and it doesn't take a huge amount of time or focus. It's found in detail in Sandra Felton's excellent book *The Messie Manual*.

The Mount Vernon Method

1. Start your cleaning at the front door.

2. Work your way around the house, room-by-room.

3. In each room, do simple dusting, once-over polishing, sweeping or vacuuming, wiping down all surfaces, putting things away, and making beds. A room is finished when its appearance is neat and its interior is clean.

4. When one room is done, proceed to the next.

5. Don't try to do the whole house in one day. Spread it out over two or three days once a month.

This system will not root out all the accumulated clutter, nor is it appropriate for heavy cleaning. But once the clutter is cleared out, the Mount Vernon method will keep clutter from ever accumulating again.

As a rule of thumb, if you are taking more than one hour per room and the rooms have been decluttered, you are probably cleaning too heavily, getting distracted, or going into micro-focus. The tendency for Marge and others with ADD is to overdo it, so pace yourself.

Three-box De-cluttering

1. Give-away box

2. Throw-away box

3. Transport box

Take three labeled boxes with you on your journey around the house: a give-away box, a throw-away box, and a transport box. The transport box is key. It is for stuff you find that does not belong in that room and needs to be transported to another room. Tossing it into the box keeps you from jumping up to take each misplaced item into another room, an act sure to break your concentration.

Routines for Dishwashing

Assuming you have an automatic dishwasher, the trick to managing dirty the dishes lies in thinking of the sink as a rinsing station and your dishwasher as a holding station. Dirty dishes get rinsed in the sink and put in the dishwasher, held until you turn the dishwasher on. If you use the sink to hold your dirty dishes rather than your dishwasher, you're sunk! Naturally, there will be times when the dirty dishes come so fast and furious that you'll need to hold them in the sink for some period of time before they go in the dishwasher. But remember this: the longer they are unrinsed in the sink, the harder they are to clean in the dishwasher. Can't keep track of turning the dishwasher on? Tie it to a nightime habit. Turn out the lights, turn on the security alarm, turn on the dishwasher.

The second roadblock in dishwashing routine is a dishwasher full of clean dishes that hasn't been unloaded. Typically, dirty dishes begin to accumulate, once again in the sink. For your system to work, you need to have a set time for unloading clean dishes.

In a busy work day schedule, mornings are often too busy for unloading clean dishes. If so, a workable weekday system is to rinse breakfast dishes, leaving them in the sink. Then, unload clean dishes during preparation of the evening meal so that your dishwasher is empty, ready for breakfast and dinner dishes. Just turn on the dishwasher after the kitchen is clean and you've completed the day's cycle.

- A.M. —rinse dishes, leave in sink
- P.M. —empty clean dishes from dishwasher before dinner
- —load day's daily dishes after dinner
- —turn on dishwasher

Routines for the Mail

The mail always comes. Rain or shine, dark of night, heat of summer, and cold of winter. Nothing keeps the mail away except Sundays and holidays. Because it is a daily and perpetual issue, it must be contended with each day—or at the very least, every two days. Here is an organized, systematic way to process your mail each day. Following this system should allow you to deal with your mail in less than five minutes each day.

1. Create a mail center

A mail center should contain:

- A trash bin or recycle bin
- Containers for each family member—clearly labeled
- Four separate "important mail" container labeled:
  1. bills
  2. action items
  3. phone calls
  4. file

Your mail center should be centrally located and convenient, placed where you and all family members can easily see and retrieve your mail. Organize your mail center so that you can stand in one spot while sorting the mail, with a trash or recycle bin in front of you, and slots or containers for each category of mail within easy reach. Often, it's most convenient to create a mail center housed on shelves hanging directly above the trash or recycle bin.

2. Sort and distribute mail in the following fashion:

- *First, sort magazines, newsletters, and catalogues.*

  This lessens the bulk of the mail dramatically. Only keep catalogues if you plan to order from them right away. Otherwise, toss them. You'll receive another within six weeks, and online ordering is always at your fingertips if you need an item before the next catalogue arrives.

- *Second, sort third class junk mail.*

  Open only the third class or junk mail if you are ready to use it. If it is an offer for a new charge card, *and you are in the market for a new charge card,* open it. If it is an offer for a new mortgage loan at a low rate, *and your are in the market for a new mortgage loan,* open it. No need to keep it "just in case" because the offer will likely expire before your need to take advantage of it arises, and you will receive new offers regularly. Toss out unopened junk mail.

▌ *Third, sort and distribute mail addressed to others.*

If you are the official "mail sorter," try to have an agreement with everyone in the family that you have their permission to toss out junk mail addressed to them. Otherwise, their accumulated clutter will work against your organizing system.

▌ *Fourth, sort the "important mail" into one of four categories:*

You will need to have a slot or container for each of the four categories of "important mail." Unlike other mail, "important mail" processing requires one more step—taking it from the sorting container to the container or file where you store or process all items of this category.

1. Bills to pay

2. Action items

Action items are those that require a written response—a letter or the completion and return of a form. These need a slot or container during sorting, but should be immediately removed to your action file.

3. Phone calls

These are items that require a phone call. While you sort your mail, these items need to be stored in a container or slot, but they should be immediately removed to wherever you keep your list of phone calls to make. This could be your to-do list or a container beside the phone.

4. Important documents to file

These "important papers" fall into a must-file category, such as insurance documents, tax documents, bank statements, and so forth.

▌ *Last and* most important, *take the four categories of "important mail" and place them where you process them,* i.e., bills in your bill paying kit, action items in your action folder,

CHAOS

phone call items in your list of calls to make or near your phone, and important documents filed in the appropriate folders.

This system may *sound* complicated, but once you've set up a convenient mail center, you'll be surprised how quickly it goes. Mail processing won't work, however, unless you have already established places for bills, action items, and important papers. (If you don't have a good system established, with a definite place for bills, action items, and file folders for important documents, refer to Chapters 17, 18, and 19 for ADD-friendly paper-management systems.)

ADD-friendly tip

If the space in your house allows it, it's most convenient to organize your home so that a desk where bills are paid, business letters are written, and documents are filed is convenient to your mail center. That way, it's one easy last step to take your "important mail" and place it where it belongs.

ADD-friendly warning

Your system will fall apart if you carefully complete the first four steps of mail processing, but fail to complete the final and most important step—taking bills, action items, and important documents to the spot where you process them. If the desk where you "take care of business" is far from your mail center, you'll be tempted to let these most important mail items pile up instead of immediately taking them to the file or container where they belong.

Level Two Solutions:	*Conquering the*
Help from Friends and Family	*Backlog of Clutter*

Backlogged residential clutter is possible to organize and get rid of, but it takes the hard work of you and at least one other person. Use the three-box technique or the Mount Vernon method described above, and enlist your clutter companion as an assistant (remember, if you have no friend or family member to serve as a clutter companion, hire a professional organizer to help you).

This time, instead of starting at the front door and working your way around to each room, pick the room that is most challenging to you. Getting that room behind you will make decluttering the rest of the house seem easier. With the help of your clutter companion, break the room down into smaller parts. A crammed closet, one side of a room, or a messy desk are good-size chunks of disorganized rooms to take on. Concentrating on perfecting each shelf of a closet or each drawer in the desk will be too "micro" to give yourself a sense of accomplishment, whereas trying to do the whole home office or the entire guest bedroom is clearly too "macro." You'll just get overwhelmed. *Doability* is the operative word here. Pick parts of the room that are doable, that you will be able to organize with success. Your clutter companion can help you set doable goals and provide support that keeps you going.

Level Three Solutions: Help from Professionals
Integrating Therapy and Organizing

Marge became increasingly aware of the interlocking influences of ADD and a disordered environment. The more she was able to take charge of ADD patterns—such as chronic sleep deprivation, poor time management, and lack of daily life-management routines—the better prepared she was to reduce the chaos in her life. The more calm and ordered her environment became, the easier it became to control her ADD symptoms.

With the structure and support of a PO, she was able to implement strategies that her ADD patterns had undermined in the past. Through a combination of therapy and working with a professional organizer she made consistent progress in changing the daily living patterns that had so strongly interfered with her professional and personal life.

Review

- Know when ADD treatment must precede organizing efforts.

- End the daily cycle of ADD disorganization.

- Increase sleep to reduce chaos.

- Counteract seasonal affective disorder.

- Build routines to reduce chaos.

- Eliminate the clutter of half-completed tasks.

- Establish routines for laundry, household cleaning, and dishes.

- Establish routines for processing mail on the spot.

- Conquer the backlog of clutter.

- Integrate therapy and organizing strategies.

Packrat Syndrome

Lois is known for her big heart. She is a generous person, eager to share her possessions with anyone in need. Throughout her sixty years, Lois' neighbors could count on her for tablecloths, wrapping paper, or screws and bolts of any shape and size. Her grandchildren have plenty of scrap paper to draw on. And every time they visit, it seems that there is another little porcelain figurine to discover. All the surfaces in Lois' home are covered with things other people might need someday. A true "people person," she saves every gift anyone has ever given her. That explains the exotic vinegars, herb pots, and multiple salt and pepper shakers that crowd her kitchen counters. Totes, handbags, luggage, plastic rain caps, tiny sewing kits, and all sorts of travel supplies cram her closets, though Lois herself only travels once or twice a year. "You just never know when someone might need these things," Lois explains.

Lois doesn't seem to be bothered by her clutter on a day-to-day basis, but her home is rapidly becoming unwelcoming to others. Friends and family have a way of visiting only briefly, if at all. Her home does not permit ease of movement and is filled with things that could be easily knocked over. It's only when company is coming, or when something really important has been misplaced, that Lois feels compelled to do any organizing.

Lois had never heard of ADD until her daughter, Mary, told her that Lois' grandson Nathan was recently diagnosed. "He can't find his homework, his desk is the messiest in school, and he saves everything! He's in the second grade and already has saved all his schoolwork, drawings, and books from first grade," Mary says. "Sounds like the poor thing is a packrat like his grandma," Lois bemoans.

John is another packrat with ADD, a collector of items large and small. While Lois hangs on to things, John actively and frequently collects things—*large* things. John has not one canoe, but several. The scoutmaster of his son's troop was selling his canoe at a rock-bottom price and John couldn't resist. With two canoes in the family, now he and his son can go canoeing on weekends, he reasons. John can't pass a neighborhood yard sale without picking up a tool, a piece of hardware, or lumber that he knows will "come in handy." "And, for only two dollars, how can I pass it up?" he asks. Like many adults with ADD, John has many enthusiasms, and an unrealistic sense of the time available to actually use the items he frequently acquires. For years there had been no room for cars in his two-car garage. Now John is talking about building a huge storage shed in the backyard to house more of his overflowing collection of items.

A "packrat" is someone who can't bear to part with things, even things with little practical use or value. Certainly, not all packrats have ADD, but there are several common ADD patterns that can lead to being a packrat:

- difficulty with decision-making—what to discard, what to keep;

- inertia—never taking action until prompted by a "crisis";

- oblivion—never noticing the accumulated clutter;

- adding without subtracting—when impulse overrides reason;

- procrastination—leading to the clutter of incomplete projects; and

- too many interests, too little time.

Indecision

Although Lois defends her clutter collecting on the grounds of thrift and charity, the real driving force behind this pattern may be a difficulty making decisions. Over the years, when faced with nagging complaints about her clutter, she defended herself, saying, "This will come in handy someday. Just wait and see." Then, feeling triumphant when she eventually finds a need for one saved item or another, her pattern is further reinforced. Lois has made a virtue of her vice. But Lois' tendency to hang on to things has become a real dilemma, undermining her quality of life. For years she has lived in a cluttered environment in which it is hard for her to function, in which it is increasingly difficult for her family to visit her.

> **➤ If decision-making is not your strength, accumulating things will be your weakness.**

When you're not sure what to do with something, the "default decision" will be to hang on to it.

Inertia

Struggling with inertia is a common ADD phenomenon. If nothing prompts an adult with ADD into action, he or she is unlikely to initiate an organizing project. For many with ADD, if it doesn't have to be done *now*, it doesn't have to be done. Individuals with ADD tend to react to external events rather than to internal initiative. The clutter that is always there becomes so familiar that you don't react to it at all. Then, some change or external event suddenly demands a reaction, drawing you out of inertia. One client with ADD required such an extreme event or "critical mass" that it took the threat of eviction by his landlord to throw him into organizing overdrive.

Critical mass is when things accumulate to a point where the clutter reaches a crisis proportion that demands action. Actions and decisions are put off until some external event forces the issue. The decision is made for you, for example, waiting until you can't open the door before removing the clutter piled behind it. Hanging on to clutter to the point of critical mass may look like a *breakdown* of an organizing system, but in actuality it *is* a system, though not a very functional one.

Lois says, "I don't pay much attention to the clutter. Then, something triggers me. It might be that I'm unable to find an important piece of paper, or that huge pile of magazines has grown so tall that it collapses in the hall and I can't walk around it anymore."

Oblivion

Lois explains, "My piles have been there for so long that they are just part of the landscape, like tables and chairs. Then, when I'm about to have someone over to my house, I step back and see the clutter the way someone else would, and I'm horrified."

John's oblivion was so great that his wife was driven to desperation. Her nagging and complaints had been completely ineffective in getting him to pick up after himself. John loves to tell the story about his wife's ultimate solution. "One day, when I arrived home from work, I sat down on the couch, as usual. I put my feet up on the coffee table, getting ready to watch the news. I tried to shove the accumulated clutter aside with my foot, but it wouldn't move. Leaning over to inspect, I saw that everything had been stapled to the coffee table, right where I'd left it the night before. As I stood up to walk across the room, I noticed that everything was stapled right where I'd left it—to the carpet, to the stairs, to the kitchen chairs. She'd finally found a way to get my attention!"

Adding without Subtracting

Not only was John oblivious to the clutter, but he also had the strong ADD tendency to *add* without *subtracting*. John, an enthusiastic accumulator—never stopping to consider whether he'd actually have time to use or enjoy the latest acquisition. Acquisition (*adding*), for those with ADD, is often done on impulse. Discarding (*subtracting*), however, is a greater challenge because there's no prompt to discard, as there is to acquire. For example, John may pass by a neighborhood yard sale and spot a set of metal storage shelves for sale—a stimulus to impulsively acquire the shelves. "If I don't get it now, it will be gone," John reasons. The time-limited opportunity prompts his action. However, there is rarely a strong immediate stimulus to prompt discard. Many with ADD continue to add, while rarely subtracting.

Procrastination

Greg is an "armchair handyman" with ADD. He has lots of experience doing household repairs and home remodeling projects. With his busy schedule and poor time management, he often starts a project, but then leaves it unfinished for a year or two while his wife fumes and complains. Each incomplete project is, of course, accompanied by accumulated clutter—paint cans, tools, lumber, electrical fixtures, hardware. Not only does Greg procrastinate in completing projects, but he insists upon leaving the clutter of materials in sight as a reminder, telling his wife, "If I put everything away, I'll never get around to finishing the project."

Too Many Interests, Too Little Time

Many adults with ADD have wide-ranging interests, with their focus shifting rapidly from one to the next. Prompted by a friend, Anne registered for a quilting course, acquiring several books, magazines, a new sewing machine, and piles of fabric scraps for her quilting project. As winter turned to spring, Anne's interest shifted to gardening. Abandoning the quilt project, she began to purchase gardening supplies and materials. A time management class at work sparked her interest and she purchased not one, but half a dozen books on time management, all of which remained on her bedside table, unread, as her focus of interest shifted yet again. Her multiple interests, and rapid shifts from one to the next, had led her environment to become chronically and increasingly cluttered. Magazines related to each of her interests continued to arrive in the mail, which she would set aside for future reading.

Level One Solutions: Ways to Help Yourself

Go for Quality over Quantity

If you are an excessive saver, and have trouble with decision-making, focus your attention on one decision only, the decision to save only the best. Quality over quantity works especially well with items you have in redundant supply. Twenty containers of oregano, nine spools of black thread, two sets of encyclopedias are not uncommon among packrats. The freshest oregano, the best spool of black thread, and the most recent encyclopedia would be the quality thing to save. If items are nearly identical, save only one. As an excessive saver, your new mottos for off-loading clutter are:

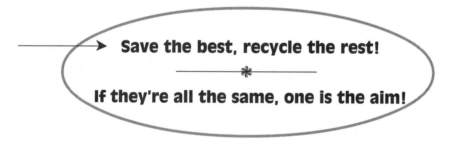

Save the best, recycle the rest!

If they're all the same, one is the aim!

Mottos like these provide you with structure, a guideline for rapid decision-making.

Create a "Crisis" to Stimulate Decluttering

Adults with ADD are more likely to act when there is an external stimulus. Create a strong signal that will tell you it's time to organize— this is an example of working *with* your ADD to get organized.

- Invite company over—creating a clean-up deadline.

- Join a block yard sale—creating a deadline for decluttering and tagging items for sale.

- Collect unread magazines in a small basket; when they spill over, that's your cue to sort and toss.

- Save unsorted mail in a wall pocket. When you can't stuff another thing in, it's time to go through it.

The Ripening Drawer Strategy

You probably have a ripening drawer or something like it right now. It's that place where you stuff things away that you are not quite ready to toss out. Things tossed in a ripening drawer are of low consequence. Not much will happen if the wrong decision is made, or even if no decision is made at all! It is a netherworld between trash and to-do. But the real magic of the ripening drawer is that when you look through it again a week from now or a month from now, it will suddenly become crystal clear whether an item is trash or a keeper. The ambiguity resolves itself.

Lois' ripening drawer contains pens that may or may not be working, used greeting cards, small miscellaneous parts, audio cassette tapes without the cases, batteries, loose change, and coupons. When she opens the drawer to add new items, she is able to quickly discard a few unwanted items to make room for the new ones. Items that Lois can't decide upon remain in the drawer. "I just can't deal with these right now," she says. No problem. That's what the ripening drawer is for. There are only two rules:

1. Do not put bills, anything to do with money, or anything with a deadline in the ripening drawer

2. Never stuff the drawer so full that it's difficult to open.

Containing your small decisions in a small space gets them out of your way so they don't distract you from other things. Each time you toss something new into the ripening drawer, look for a couple of "ripe" items to toss out.

Adding and Subtracting

If you're prone to ADD-ition—constantly bringing possessions into your life—add a new guideline to your life as well. Make a two-for-one rule: for every item you add, you'll subtract at least two. If a new magazine arrives in the mail, toss two before adding it to your collection. If you purchase new clothing, toss two items that you rarely wear. Items don't necessarily need to be the same category. Just stick to the rule:

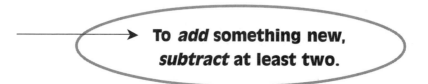

To *add* something new, *subtract* at least two.

When your addition is related to a serious collection—record albums, books, pottery, artwork—set a rule that you won't add a new item to your collection before you create an attractive, practical storage space in which to keep it. In other words, no more piling books on the floor beside the chock-full bookcase. You'll need to either purchase a new bookcase or discard books to make room for the new ones.

Make Room for the Future

Hanging on to the clutter of past projects is often related to feelings of shame and regret—shame that you didn't live up to your declarations (This year, I'm going to get in shape.), regret that you didn't have the discipline to master a skill (I'm going to learn to play that guitar). As long as you hang on to the guitar or rowing machine, you tell yourself, you'll get around to it eventually. By giving them away, you feel you're admitting defeat.

One constructive way to deal with the clutter of abandoned interests is to embrace this aspect of yourself. Anticipate and accept your pattern of short-term interests. Look for less-expensive used equipment, then resell it for little or no loss and move on to your next interest without guilt or regret.

Another constructive way to rid yourself of clutter is to frame it in terms of making room for the future. Individuals with ADD tend to crave stimulation, a craving that may send you forward, into new interests and adventures, instead of sticking with previous interests. If you're an adult with ADD who belongs to the "School of What's Happening Now," you need to make room for what interests you *now* by clearing out relics from your past.

Set a Deadline for Project Completion

If some of your clutter is related to never-finished projects, set a deadline for project completion, with a promise to yourself (and the people that you live with) that you'll toss it if you haven't used it by the deadline. Make the deadline realistic, but soon enough to create a sense of urgency. For example: I'll finish that sewing project by my niece's birthday and give it to her as a gift.

ADD-Friendly Habits to Combat the Collection of Clutter

1. *Reward yourself with experiences instead of things.* Many people with ADD reward themselves by purchasing clothing, books, magazines, or gadgets. If you're feeling down, instead of shopping, develop other ways to give your mood a boost—a massage, a hot bath, time with a friend, a movie.

2. *Guard the door!* Become super-vigilant about what comes in the door. If it doesn't enter your home, it can't become clutter. Magazines, newspapers, junk mail, and casual purchases have a way of permanently populating your tables and counters if you let them in the door.

3. *Make throw-away/give-away into a daily habit.* Keep a box or bag in a storage area to collect give-away items. As you notice an item that you don't want or use, immediately take it to the give-away bag or box. Don't let unwanted or unused items take up valuable space waiting for a periodic dig-out. Place small throw-away items in the trash, and larger ones in a storage area for trash pick-up day.

Level Two Solutions:	*Set a Deadline*
Help from Friends and Family	*with a Family Member*

Projects that lie incomplete, cluttering areas of the home used by others, can lead to tension and annoyance. "Are you *ever* going to finish that?" Setting a deadline with consequences can be very effective for adults with ADD.

Sometimes adults with ADD begin to clutter the common areas of their home because their "own" space is too cluttered to use. This is the case for Art. He had an office upstairs so filled with clutter that he has developed the habit of doing paperwork on the dining room table. Soon, his clutter migrates to such an extent that the dining room table is no longer a clear, distraction-free area for him to work.

Art and his wife are both learning about ADD and how to find ADD-friendly strategies to reduce clutter. Art recognizes that he works better with deadlines, but rarely keeps deadlines that he sets for himself. Working with his wife, they both agree that he can *temporarily* continue to use the dining room—but only if he agrees to gather his papers into a letter basket at the end of each evening. They also agree upon a second deadline—that Art will declutter his office by month's end, so that the dining room table will no longer become his office annex. If the office remains cluttered at the end of the month, Art agrees to dedicate that weekend to an office dig-out, allowing his wife to be his clutter companion during the dig-out. Because Art never wants anyone else interfering with his "private space," the end-of-the-month deadline is one he takes seriously.

For Greg and Linda, incomplete home repair and remodeling projects were a chronic problem. They also agreed to deadlines with consequences. For each incomplete project Greg—who has ADD—sets a realistic completion deadline. He agrees that if the deadline passes without project completion, his wife can hire someone to finish the job. Soon, projects were being completed—some by Greg, and others by professionals. Clutter began to vanish, to their joint satisfaction.

 ### Decide when "Someday" Is

How often have you said, "I'll get around to cleaning

this place out someday?" But you don't have to wait until someday comes. You have the power to decide when someday is. By making a commitment to a clutter companion, you'll have more structure and support, so that someday really arrives and your decluttering happens. Here is how it's done.

1. **Pick a date in the future**—any date thirty to ninety days away. Choose a date that works for both your schedule and that of your clutter companion. Any longer than that, and you will be living in too much clutter; any shorter than that, and you might feel like someday is closing in on you too fast.

2. **On your calendar write "Someday" on the date you have chosen.** Now you've actually designated when someday is.

3. **Choose a date one week before someday, and write "Get supplies"** on that date on your calendar. That day, purchase the supplies that you'll need, including empty boxes, plastic bags, file folders, or other organizing supplies. You may want to discuss supplies with your clutter companion as he or she is usually experienced in planning a dig-out day.

4. **On the day before someday, write "Prepare" on your calendar.** Prepare by purchasing food and drinks that will be on hand for the big day. Go to bed early and get plenty of sleep. Plan to rise and eat breakfast well before the hour you've set to begin. Organizing can be hard work, physically and mentally.

5. **Spend someday with your clutter companion, deciding what to give away and throw away.** Place items for charity pick-up in large plastic bags, labeled and placed out of the way. Throw-away items should leave the house that day—out to the trash cans, larger items taken to the dump. Give as many items as you can to friends, family, and neighbors, but don't let the give-away process prolong your dig-out process.

6. **You won't get it all done, so plan another someday in two or three months.**

Declutter as a Family

Decluttering can be a lonely, tiresome task, but doing it as a family can be much easier, and even fun. Remember:

To get it done, make it fun!

Make decluttering a regular, monthly family event. Instead of nagging family members about their mess, and feeling guilty about your own, organize the "clutter Olympics." Offer a prize to the family member who collects the most throw-away and give-away items in one hour. Give prizes for speed, endurance, and clutter poundage.

Level Three Solutions:	*Put a Professional*
Help from Professionals	*Organizer on Your*
	Organizing Team

When your decluttering strategies haven't been effective, and even after asking for help from a clutter companion your home is still in great disorder, then it's time to call in a professional organizer. A professional organizer makes a living getting others organized. When clutter causes chaos, a PO can inject order and systems. A PO will work with you on-site at your home, helping you decide what to keep and what to toss, and making sure you stay on task. You'll find that your morale will be higher and the work will go faster. POs will also have ideas for getting organized you probably never thought of and that will keep you stimulated.

Decide Who "Somebody" Is

One creative idea, developed by a PO, is to decide who "Somebody" is—that unnamed somebody that you're saving everything for—because

"Somebody" might need it some day. Instead of saving for "Somebody," your PO can help you decide who "Somebody" actually is. This will target your saving for specific people rather than saving for an ambiguous recipient called "Somebody."

You will need a supply of removable small adhesive labels available from any stationary or office supply store. Don't buy an excessive amount. One package contains hundreds of labels and it will do you fine.

1. Walk through your home and think about exactly who should be the recipients of the items you are saving. Come up with a real name of a real person. Use your professional organizer to help you think it through.

2. Write the person's name on a label and affix the label to an unobtrusive part of the item, like inside a shirt cuff, or on the bottom of a lamp.

3. Have your PO make an extra label for every one you write and affix it to a sheet of paper entitled "Someday."

4. Try to assign every item you are saving to an actual person. If nobody's name comes to mind, write "needy person" on the label and affix it to the item.

5. By the time you are done, each saved article will have an intended recipient, and you will also have a list of intended recipients on the list called "Someday."

6. Take out your calendar and plan "someday" as described earlier. Use your PO to help you.

7. Invite the recipients to come by on your someday. Explain to the recipients that you are doing some organizing and have some things for them and you'd love them to come by.

8. Call a local charity, and arrange a pick-up at the end of some-day so that anything remaining, including articles labeled "needy person," can be donated.

9. After someday has come and gone, whenever you save something for somebody be certain to label it right away.

> **Always contact a charity that does free pick-ups so you won't have to load, transport, and unload the remaining stuff yourself.**

Play Friends, Acquaintances, and Strangers

Conventional methods for decluttering require you to divorce yourself emotionally from your possessions. But people who save excessively can sometimes benefit from just the opposite, from exaggerating your attachment to your possessions. In the process of exaggerating your feelings for your things, it becomes clearer what you really care about and what you do not. This clarity enables you to discard with ease those things you no longer care much about without a lot of decision-making.

 You'll find your clutter companion or PO helpful because they will help you make fast choices, and also because it's more fun with someone else!

Friends, Acquaintances, Strangers

1. Clear a table, counter, or other waist-high surface for sorting.

> **Always sort waist-high.**
> **Sorting low on the floor**
> **or high on a shelf is hard on your back**
> **and will contribute to your**
> **resistance to sorting.**

2. Collect a bunch of items of a similar type that you want to sort—for instance, a bunch of books, a stack of clothes, or the entire contents of a kitchen cabinet.

3. Set them on the sorting table.

4. Select about a third of all the items as your "friends." Don't worry how to define "friend." Your friends could be your nicest clothes, or your favorite clothes, or the ones that look best on you, or any combination. Just go with your gut.

5. Keep your friends. Put them away right now.

6. Select about a third as "strangers." Again, how you define stranger is up to you. It could be clothes you know you will never wear, or the ones you don't even remember having, or the ones that don't fit, or any combination. Go with your gut.

7. Toss the strangers out! A large plastic bag right into the garbage is best, unless you care to donate them.

8. You are left with your "acquaintances." Acquaintances come into your life and usually pass through it, not staying too long. Acquaintances need to be donated. Put the acquaintances in a large plastic bag and put it in your car right now.

Packrat Syndrome

Use a PO and a Crew

If you have accumulated a large quantity of stuff that makes you feel overwhelmed just looking at it, you might need a crew to make a fast, long-lasting difference. A crew consists of you (the owner of the clutter), a PO supervisor, and at least one assistant. Your PO can locate an assistant. Together, they will presort your things according to your presort categories:

- clothing;
- books;
- loose papers;
- unopened mail;
- photographs;
- stationary supplies; and
- recommended refuse (recommended by your PO).

You don't have to use these presort categories, but they are pretty common. Of all the presort categories, the most important is recommended refuse. Your PO and assistant are not allowed to throw any of your things away, even if they obviously look like trash. But they will put these things aside for you to review in a stack called "recommended refuse." It's your job to determine if these items should be trashed, donated, recycled, or kept.

Many people with ADD find the commotion of a crew a great relief. It creates an atmosphere of activity and productivity and capitalizes on your need for stimulation. However, there are also people with ADD who find commotion very distracting and unsettling. If you know yourself to be one of these people, a crew might not be your best option. You may be more comfortable working only with your PO.

Consider Psychological Help

Look out for warning signs of emotional or psychological obstacles to your organizing. These include:

■ making a decision to throw something away and then retrieving the item from the garbage;

■ an overwhelming feeling of grief or sadness when you throw
something away;

■ a total paralysis that prevents you from making any organizing decisions at all; or

■ a declining level of sanitation or safety in your home.

If you experience any of these, speak with your therapist or doctor.
If you do not have a therapist or doctor, call your local mental health
association. These patterns signal a problem that might require
counseling or medical attention.

Review

■ Recognize that your packrat patterns may be due to ADD.

■ Go for quality over quantity.

■ Use organizing signals.

■ Have a ripening drawer.

■ Plan a reason to organize.

■ Reward yourself with experiences rather than things.

■ Guard the door! Don't let the clutter in.

■ Make throw-away/give-away into a daily habit.

■ Put a clutter companion on your organizing team.

■ Decide when "someday" is.

■ Decide who "somebody" is.

■ Put a professional organizer on your organizing team.

■ Play friends, acquaintances, and strangers.

■ Use a crew.

■ Consider psychological help.

Chapter **Twelve**

David's Garage

David's garage is a nightmare. The cars are parked outside on the street because the tools, sporting equipment, old paint cans, and half-finished projects crowd the garage so much that the only item related to transportation that fits is a thin bicycle. When the garage door is lifted, something always shifts a little, threatening to tumble to the ground. If it were up to David, he might never change the way his garage is organized. "Messy as this garage is, believe it or not I know where everything is. I'd be afraid to move anything, because once I did I'm sure I'd never be able to find it again."

According to David's wife, Rebecca, David is missing the whole point. "Sure, he can find anything when he wants to, but it takes him forever, and *I* can't find a thing!" she exclaims. "And I don't want to have to ask David to find things for me. A garage is supposed to be self-service. Last week I bought a new flashlight because I couldn't find one. Do you know we have four flashlights in that garage? If the garage were better organized, we'd know what we have and would be able to store more. Also, I hate the way it looks. David could care less."

Dave's "organization" of the garage just evolved. He didn't plan it. Most of the paint cans are in one far corner of the garage, but the off-white semigloss is near the door. He stuck it there when he used it last. As he crawls around the chaos in the garage, he develops a visual image. "The bike pump is over there, near the rolled-up carpet remnant," he recalls. Although Dave claims he can find anything, it's really not as easy as he says. His wife has a point. If he knows where everything is, why does he own four flashlights?

Like many with ADD, Dave's memory system doesn't rely on organization and categories, such as large tools hanging on the wall, small tools in the tool box. It relies on visual memory. "I know the monkey wrench is somewhere over there," David says to himself, "I can just 'see' it in my mind, somewhere on these shelves near the paint rags and sandpaper."

Part of the conflict between David and his wife may have as much to do with personality as with ADD. Not all people, with or without ADD, place neatness and order high on their value list (for example, the woman who humorously places a magnet on her refrigerator door that proclaims, "A well-kept home is the sign of a wasted life"). Not only does David have difficulty being orderly (an ADD-related trait), but he doesn't feel

> ### Is this your story?
> ### It is if you:
>
> ■ can find things if you dig a while, but keep everything in a jumble;
>
> ■ tend to have a big picture rather than detailed view of things; and
>
> ■ have tried to get organized but can't.

that his disorder is a significant problem (a personality-related trait). David's primary motivation to organize is to please his wife. If his efforts are to succeed, his approach to organizing will need to be one that appeals to David's creative, off-beat personality. Otherwise, he'll feel that he's been placed in a straightjacket and will soon rebel.

Level Three Solutions: Help from Professionals

The same approaches can't work for everyone. For example, Marge, in Chapter 10, who suffered from the CHAOS, couldn't benefit from organizing assistance until she had received treatment for her ADD. In David's case, strategies to help himself, or to organize with the help of family and friends are unlikely to work for several reasons. The organizing job he is confronting with is too big. David is resistant to organizing. *And* David has ADD.

David needs to start with professional organizing help. Without a professional organizer, he's unlikely to succeed. A professional organizer who is familiar with ADD can also assist his wife and other family members in better understanding ADD. If family members can learn ADD-friendly organizing strategies, they will be more successful in supporting David in maintenance organizing tasks after a professional organizer has helped him create order.

Use a Big-Picture Approach

Jane, in Chapter 9, found that breaking things down was helpful because she felt easily overwhelmed by surveying an entire room. David, however, does not feel overwhelmed by his clutter. In fact, he's rather comfortable with it. In addition, he's a big-picture person, more interested in themes and ideas than details.

Instead of breaking things down, as Jane did, David needs to do just the opposite. He needs to develop an organizing theme that encompasses his entire garage. An overall theme can give an organizing project a big-picture backdrop. David, in collaboration with his PO, chooses a hardware store theme for organizing his garage.

Use Creativity as a Motivator

In addition to being a big-picture thinker, David is creative and loves to do things in an off-beat way. The idea of organizing is very unappealing to David. Instead of associating organization with creativity, for him, being orderly has connotations of tedium and rigidity. David's professional organizer is using a very ADD-friendly strategy—finding an ADD motivator, in this case, creativity—to enhance the appeal of an organizing task. To David, developing a hardware store theme in his garage feels like an enjoyable, creative challenge rather than a boring, tedious task he's undertaking just to please his wife.

Developing the Hardware Store Theme

A hardware store is organized into departments like the tool department, paint department, sporting goods, and so forth. David organized his tool department first. With his PO as supervisor, David and his kids pull tools from the clutter. They pick up tools from the floor, grab them from the shelves above, and gather them from every hiding place in the garage. David has a grand old time amassing all the

Other Organizing Themes You Can Use	
Organizing Project	**Possible Themes**
Home office ⟶	The war room Communications center
Kid's room ⟶	A board game Mini-apartment
Kitchen ⟶	A restaurant or Inn The command center
Garage ⟶	A hardware store Mini "Home" Depot
The Den ⟶	Alpine lounge Entertainment center

Creative Organizing

tools together in a great big pile on the garage floor, tossing away broken ones as he goes.

David's fifteen-year-old son has been given the job of organizing the paint department. He is enthusiastic (he is being paid by the hour) searching out paint cans, locating all the brushes, dragging over ladders, and gathering together turpentine cans, rags, and everything else having to do with painting. Even David's twelve-year-old daughter gets into the act. She is on a treasure hunt for sporting equipment. She finds all the old skis, baseballs, tennis rackets, and golf clubs and brings them together into a heap on the floor.

As paint brushes, tennis rackets, and screwdrivers hurtle through the air to their appointed separate piles on the garage floor, Rebecca grows increasingly anxious. The garage is looking worse than ever. David doesn't seem to be fazed at all by the deconstruction of the garage.

Now that David (with his family) has deconstructed the garage and eliminated the broken and unuseable stuff, he needs a model for organizing his hardware store, a visual model that he can use as a starting point. So off David, his PO, and Rebecca go to the local hardware store. Of course, the *real* hardware store has more inventory, space, and money to organize the store than David's family does, but David and Rebecca can see that inexpensive wall-mounted pegboards, simple prefabricated shelving, and large colorful plastic bins will be of great help. They take Polaroid photographs of the hardware store as a record of how its inventory is organized. David, in his typical ADD style, creates his hardware store with his family's help, in several bursts of weekend energy.

Dr. Lynn Weiss, in her book *A.D.D. and Success*, writes, of a client similar to David, that organizing takes place in the "creative mind," outside of consciousness, born whole. This creative organizing style is contrasted to the more linear style of planning and breaking a task down into steps to be accomplished one at a time. Weiss writes that neither organizing style is better; they're just different.

David, unlike some people with ADD, is energized by the chaos that develops in the process of completing a creative task. He is able to tolerate chaos for long periods of time while the chaos undergoes a transformation to something new. David can organize if he experiences organizing as building something new instead of breaking something down. And if that creating something new causes more chaos in the process, so be it.

Drs. Ned Hallowell and John Ratey, in their book on attention deficit disorder *Driven to Distraction,* write:

> In order to arrange life, in order to create, one must get comfortable with disarrangement for a while. One must be able to live with the unfamiliar. . . . In bearing with the tension of the unknown or the unfamiliar, one can enable something new to come into existence. (p. 177)

David is not only able to live with the unfamiliar, he thrives on it. Working with the structure and support of a professional organizer who developed strategies that worked *with* David's ADD and creative bent, David was able to enthusiastically engage in the organizing project and follow it through to completion.

Review

- Use an organizing style that fits both your ADD and your personality.

- Use creativity as a motivation for organizing.

- When a detail approach to organizing doesn't suit, try a big-picture approach.

- Choose an organizing theme to add both structure and creative appeal to your organizing task.

Part *Four*

Time Organizing

Time Out

Phyllis and her daughter, Kelly, both have ADD. Temporarily between jobs, Phyllis would like to use this time to get better organized. "I finally have time to organize the house and finish my overdue taxes. Two or three months at home will be heaven." Phyllis has a list of about fifty to-do items, a day planner, and a commitment to put the most important things first in her life: her daughter, her health, and spending time with friends. All the elements of a well-organized person seem to be in place, and yet . . .

Today Phyllis is at her kitchen table, where she starts her day with a cup of coffee and the mail. The newspaper catches her eye, and she reads the front page; pretty soon she finds herself lost in the newspaper. The phone rings, a neighbor inviting her for a walk. "Perfect," Phyllis thinks. "I can kill two birds with one stone, exercise and socializing with my friend." Forty-five minutes later, she returns from her walk, hungry, just as the phone rings again. The mother of one of Kelly's soccer teammates needs to arrange the transportation schedule for the week. While on the phone, Phyllis takes the opportunity to discuss her concern about a school policy. They hang up twenty minutes later.

Realizing she has a dentist appointment in forty-five minutes, she rushes to take a shower, quickly dresses, and grabs a pastry at the coffee shop on the way. In her haste, she has forgotten to bring any paperwork or her book, so she must settle for reading old magazines in the waiting room. A follow-up appointment will be necessary, but because her day planner is at home, Phyllis must take the dentist's card and remember to call to make another appointment. It's almost noon. She dashes to the music store to pick up a flute rental for Kelly's band class and grabs a quick lunch at a nearby café.

Kelly will be home from school in two hours, and Phyllis wants to be there for her. Driving home, she spots a dress sale and decides to look inside. "This will only take a minute," she remembers saying to herself. It doesn't seem as if she's been shopping long, but a glance at her watch throws Phyllis into a panic. She quickly pays for her purchase and rushes to the grocery store to pick up milk. She is sure other groceries are needed, but without her list, she can't recall what, and besides, she's out of time. It's 3:15, and Kelly has just gotten home from school, enthusiastic about trying her new flute. A few minutes into her practice, Kelly announces that she needs extra school supplies for tomorrow. "I just got back

> ## Is this your story?
>
> ### It is if you:
>
> ■ tend to lose track of time;
>
> ■ are poor at estimating how long a task will take;
>
> ■ have difficulty scheduling your time; and
>
> ■ feel you have little control over your use of time.

from the store!" Phyllis exclaims with annoyance in her voice. "Well, I'm sorry, Mom. I just remembered now," Kelly pleads. So with snack in hand, they get back into the car and head for the office supply store.

Returning home, it's now time to make dinner. Phyllis reflects on her annoyance with Kelly and wonders how she can become so frustrated with Kelly's forgetfulness when she herself forgets things all the time. As the evening passes, Phyllis realizes that, once again, another day has gone by without making any progress on her main goals: organizing her house and finishing her taxes. "I'm always frustrated. I'm busy all day, but I never seem to accomplish everything that I should."

ADD and Time Awareness

Several ADD tendencies complicate the time management picture so profoundly that most conventional time management advice simply does not apply to adults with ADD. Take Phyllis, for example. She tends to overestimate the time she has available to her, a typical time management mistake. Many of us do this because we fail to account for "unplanned" events like interruptions, traffic, and other events beyond our control.

But Phyllis's unrealistic sense of time is also affected by poor awareness of time itself—a trait very common to those with ADD. To Phyllis, time does not occur in neat little experiential bundles of minutes and hours. Drs. John Ratey and Ned Hallowell note that instead of being able to carve out discrete activities that would create a sensation of separate moments, for the ADD person everything runs together, unbraked, uninhibited. Because Phyllis experiences time as a constant, unpredictable flow, it is extremely difficult for her to accurately gauge the passage of time.

Interruptions

Distractibility, a hallmark trait of ADD, also plays a role in Phyllis's poor time awareness. Distractibility is the tendency to become easily sidetracked, to lose focus because your attention is pulled away from the activity in which you are engaged. Phyllis is unable to block out distractions and also has difficulty remembering to return to her task after a distraction has occurred. Even though Phyllis sets out to open the mail, her attention bounces between the mail, the ringing phone, the newspaper, a random thought, and back again to the mail (if she's lucky!). Bouncing somewhat randomly from one focus to the next, her sense of the passage of time is easily thrown off.

Internal distractions

Finally, there is the issue of internal distractions. Many people with ADD have minds that are running constantly, filled with multiple thoughts and associations. As a result, even when the external world is not distracting them they become distracted by their own thoughts. For example, Phyllis may be reading a magazine, and see an article that interests her on hand-painted ceramics. This makes her think of her friend who creates hand-painted ceramics, and suddenly Phyllis remembers that she's forgotten to call this friend about the upcoming craft fair. Jumping up to make the phone call before she forgets again, she becomes engaged in a lengthy, rambling discussion with her friend. In this sequence, Phyllis is distracting herself, jumping from one related thought or activity to the next, with no planning and little awareness of the passage of time.

Time as a series of "nows"

For many adults with ADD, life is experienced as a series of "nows." Phyllis has difficulty keeping a focus on her long-term priorities because she is continuously caught up in the "now" of her immediate experience. For a priority to receive her attention, it must become part of her immediate experience. If a priority has been planned and recorded on paper, it commands little or no attention in comparison to the "now" of the ringing telephone or interaction with her daughter.

Level One Solutions:
Ways to Help Yourself   *Pattern Planning*

Pattern planning, a time-management system recommended by Drs. John Ratey and Ned Hallowell, two well-known authorities on ADD, is an excellent way to manage your time better, instead of staying caught up in "nows." Pattern planning is a way to build structure into the course of your day, as well as a way to keep the relentless "nows" from stealing time from your priorities. Pattern planning begins with a daily pattern, then your weekly pattern is added; and, finally, monthly or irregular commitments are added.

Daily Patterns

Your daily pattern should include not only the usual daily events, but also should include regularly scheduled times to attend to your priorities. For example, if regular exercise is a priority for Phyllis, then she should develop a pattern or template for each day, selecting an exercise time that fits into her other activities. Organizing her home and completing her tax forms have also been declared top priorities, and Phyllis needs to assign regular times during each day to work on them.

Phyllis's daily pattern might look something like this:

7:00 A.M.	Get up
7:15–8:00 A.M.	Breakfast, read the paper
8:00 A.M.	Exercise: 45 minutes
8:45 A.M.	Shower and dress
9:00 A.M.	Breakfast dishes, general straightening of the house
9:30 A.M.	Household organizing (top priority): 1 hour
10:30 A.M.-noon	—
Noon	Lunch: hour
1:00–3:00	Errands
3:00 P.M.	home to meet Kelly
3:00–4:00 P.M.	Time with Kelly (top priority)
4:00-5:00 P.M.	—
5:00 P.M.	Begin dinner preparations
6:00–7:00 P.M.	Dinner with the family (top priority)
7:30–8:30 P.M.	Work on taxes (top priority)
8:30–10:00 P.M.	—
10:00 P.M.	Get in bed to read
11:00 P.M.	Lights out

Weekly Patterns

In addition to a daily pattern, Phyllis also has regular weekly commitments. The flow of each day will vary depending upon these weekly events. Weekly events might include:

- a regularly scheduled class,
- meetings,
- chores,

- appointments (hairdresser), and

- rehearsals.

After filling out her daily pattern, Phyllis can readily see that she has four flexible hours in each day, from 10:30 A.M. to noon, from 4:00 to 5:00 P.M. from 8:30 to 10:00 P.M. To maintain her daily pattern, these are the best time slots to schedule weekly or irregular events. Of course, life never happens so neatly. When Phyllis can choose, she should make appointments for mid- to late morning. A class, a choir practice, or other activity may require flexibility in her schedule on those days. For example, she may decide that on choir practice night she will not prepare dinner, but will plan for carry-out food, allowing her time to work on her taxes in the late afternoon, since she won't be able to work on her taxes in the usually scheduled slot that evening.

Irregular Commitments

Then, irregular commitments, such as doctor or dental appointments, or social events, need to be entered into the daily pattern. Often, these irregularly scheduled events must take precedence over the standard daily pattern. To implement pattern planning, you should:

- make a list of regular daily events;

- make a list of your fixed tasks, obligations, and appointments;

- use a week-at-a-glance calendar or appointment book and plug in your fixed tasks, obligations, and appointments; and

- do this every week.

Soon you'll find that these fixed tasks will take on the character of regular appointments and will take root in your subconscious. The more you enter fixed tasks into your schedule, the less you'll need to rely on your memory, mood, or complicated planning. Also, by regularly building in blocks of time for your top-priority activities, you are more likely to move toward your goals.

Block out Unrealistic Thinking

Blocking is a visual aid that helps you *see* how much time your commitments actually take. Instead of simply writing an appointment into your calendar, write the range of time it will take and draw a bold line down from the start time to the finish time.

Instead of This	Do This
Sept. 2nd —Noon—Doctor	Sept. 2nd 11:30 Doctor 1:00

Blocking can be very helpful in dealing with unrealistic thinking. Phyllis thinks that because she is free from the demands of a full-time job right now her entire day is open to use as she wishes. In her mind she sees vistas of ten-hour days one after the other like the open plains of Kansas. With her time commitments blocked in, Phyllis can see graphically how her time is already committed and what time is actually available to her.

Work on Big Tasks in Short Spurts

Phyllis, like many people with ADD, has just the right kind of energy for accomplishing things in short spurts of time. If you work best in short spurts but have a big project to accomplish, don't unrealistically set aside a huge block of time for the task. Many people with ADD who face a large, difficult task—such as Phyllis's goal of completing past-due taxes—feel they must set aside a huge block of time because the task feels so huge. They may set aside an entire weekend, only to find that they've actually spent little time on their taxes during that block of time.

Let your attention span be your guide

If your maximum length of effective concentration on a detailed or demanding task is thirty minutes, then set your goal at thirty minutes. You'll get much more done if you work on the "big" task for half an hour every single day than you will by trying to chain yourself to your desk all day on Saturday. Set a timer for thirty minutes as you sit down to begin your task. When the timer sounds, you've accomplished your goal for that day. If you're still focused and feel that you can keep going, reset the timer for another thirty minutes.

Pick up where you left off

Many people with ADD object to working in short spurts saying that it takes them too long to figure out "where they were" each time they return to the task. The solution to this problem—at the end of each half-hour session, write yourself a note recording what you've done and what to do next.

Scheduling According to Mood

Some people with ADD have a strong aversion to living a highly scheduled life. If this is true of you, it's important that you make life choices that allow for maximum flexibility. For example, choosing work that you can do at home at any hour. Of course, there are inflexible to-do's in any life, but thoughtful lifestyle decisions can reduce the number of inflexible to-do's in your life.

Mood scheduling is more spontaneous than standard scheduling, because it involves choosing your *preferred* time for a given activity whenever possible. In this way, your to-do's are more often "want-to-do's" and less often "have-to-do's." If you have a strong preference for doing tasks according to mood, build a flexible schedule for yourself that includes:

▌ regular high-priority activities such as work, family time, life-maintenance activities, exercise, and reading;

▌ your stubby to-do list for the day—a short list of errands or tasks that are outside your everyday routine (see Chapter 8 for more on stubby to-do lists); and

■ a schedule of inflexible to-do's—those activities that *must* be done at a particular time, regardless of your mood or preference, such as a scheduled appointment or scheduled activities of family members.

Within that day's framework, you can feel free to operate according to mood. Rather do your paperwork first thing and get it over with? Go right ahead! More in the mood to do your exercise now and run errands later? No problem. A mood-driven schedule allows flexibility within the framework of the day. Do things in the order that feels best to you on that particular day, as long as you accomplish your goals by day's end.

Strengthen Your Time Sense by Staying on Task

If you rarely get to experience accomplishing something from beginning to end, you have very little to go on to figure out how long something takes to do. No wonder scheduling is such a challenge! To optimize your chances of completing a task from beginning to end, coping with distractions is key. You can accomplish this by making your intentions stronger and your distractions weaker.

Enhance your focus with an ADD-friendly environment

Set yourself up to stay focused until you reach your goal. Make what you intend to do noticeable, appealing, and compelling, and what you don't intend to do difficult and less convenient. For example, make your workspace appealing, well-lit, and uncluttered—a place you *want* to be. Don't try to work in a dark, cluttered, unappealing back bedroom or basement.

Use self-talk to get back on task

Self-talk is an excellent way to manage distractions. Whenever you have a random thought or idea that will take you off the task at hand, ask yourself out loud "Where was I?" If an external distraction takes you from one task to another to another, stop and say out loud, "What do I need to be doing right now?" The key is to say these words out loud so that your intentions are in the foreground and distractions fade to the background.

Use intention markers

An intention marker lets you know exactly where you left off when you became distracted. Because Phyllis cannot resist picking up a ringing phone, she has a small, red sticky note pad stuck right to the telephone. (Just remove the paper backing on the note pad and stick it to the phone.) Whenever the phone rings, she jots a one-word note on the sticky note and sticks it to her hand. It might say "dishes," for instance, reminding her to go back to putting the dishes away after the phone call.

Take Green Breaks to Increase Task Completion

Good time management involves not only focusing on tasks, but also scheduling breaks. Lack of task completion is a chronic problem for many adults with ADD. Typically, they work full steam ahead until they can work no longer. If the task is not yet completed, they may become distracted and have difficulty coming back to the task. Taking breaks to refresh your energy and concentration is an effective way to increase your chances of completing your task.

However, your "fifteen-minute break" may stretch far beyond its allotted time, and you may become distracted by another activity, never returning to your original task. "I'll sit down to balance my checkbook, need a break, stand up, walk inside, and next thing I know, I'm doing the laundry!" says Phyllis.

Try taking green breaks instead. A green break is a way of refreshing the brain that is brief but effective. It can be done as often as needed but won't take you far from your task. To take a green break:

1. Stand up facing something green. (A tree, a lawn, a leafy plant on a deck, or even a poster of a green pasture will do.)

2. Focus on the greenery.

3. Breathe in slowly. Feel your chest rise.

4. Exhale slowly. Let the air escape fully.

5. Breathe in again, this time bringing your arms up over your head, then lower them as you breathe out.

6. Now, drink a glass of water.

7. Finally, rock slowly from side to side.

8. Begin working again.

The color green, especially in nature, is calming. Rocking and raising your arms is relaxing, the water replenishes you, and the increased oxygen from deep breathing will make you more alert. A green break is ADD-friendly because it refreshes you, allowing you to benefit from a break without allowing you to become distracted by other things.

Reducing Distractions to Increase Task Completion

Distractions often interfere with concentration for adults with ADD. When surrounded by distractions, you have to expend more effort to concentrate and are more likely to get off task or to tire before you've completed your task. To weaken external distractions, try some of the following tips:

Reducing auditory distractions

▪ When possible, turn off the distracting sound, such as the television.

▪ When nearby conversation is distracting, use "white noise." If you work in a small cubicle surrounded by talkative people, a small white noise machine can create a sound cocoon that can block out distracting sounds and conversations.

▪ Use low volume music to block out other auditory distractions.

Reducing visual distractions

▮ Turn off the TV if you find that you frequently glance at it when working.

▮ Close the window shades if outside activity captures your attention.

▮ Clear off your work space. By eliminating the visual distractions of clutter, you will function more easily and efficiently.

▮ When you cannot block out a visual distraction, use verbalization to override the distraction. For example, if you are sorting through papers, looking for a specific item, and find yourself distracted by other papers, talk to yourself to keep on track. Say, "I'm looking for that letter I wrote to the insurance company last week." When you find something really intriguing, use self-talk—"I'll put this aside to look at in a minute. Right now, I'm looking for that letter."

▮ Sit facing away from distractions such as people passing by your doorway.

Reducing tempting distractions

▮ Turn off the phone if you can't let it ring without answering it.

▮ Leave the computer room and do your work elsewhere or work on a laptop not connected to the Internet if you can't resist surfing the web or "instant messaging" friends.

▮ Put up a "do not disturb" sign to eliminate interruptions if you have difficulty resisting conversation with coworkers.

▮ Put temptations that pull you away from your task out of sight and out of reach.

Reducing internal distractions

▮ "Capture" random ideas on sticky notes so that you can

return to your task without fear of forgetting the fleeting thought.

∎ Read aloud if you find that internal thoughts distract you from reading material that is important but uninteresting or difficult to read.

Worry Outlets

A worry outlet is a place to put things that cause you to worry when worries are getting in the way of your accomplishing your tasks. For instance, Phyllis used to worry about her credit card debt every time she opened the mail because it would always be full of credit card offers that reminded her of her own debt. She has created a worry outlet labeled "Talk to Financial Planner" on her desk. This is a vertical file in which she stores credit card offers, articles on tax advice, information on insurance and other financial matters. On her schedule, she has a standing monthly appointment with her financial planner. Now instead of worrying unproductively about these matters, she has a worry outlet, a planned meeting with her financial planner. When she goes, she grabs her file and talks these things over with her financial planner.

Phyllis has created a set of "worry outlets"—vertical files on her desk—that allow her to stay focused on her immediate tasks because she has a system for taking care of her worries. Her files are labeled:

∎ Talk to spouse

∎ Discuss with teacher

∎ Ask lawyer

∎ Tell the doctor

∎ Ask PO

∎ Talk to financial planner

You may have a different set of issues that could benefit from a "worry outlet" in your life. Setting up a place to file away your concerns, and setting up a regular time to deal with each category, can help you stay focused on the activity of the moment without being frequently distracted by free-floating worries. Making an appointment with your "worry contact"—your spouse, your child's teacher, or whomever—can reduce anxiety in the present.

Level Two Solutions:	*Use a Time Log*
Help from Friends and Family	*to Increase Your*
	Time Awareness

With the help of a time tutor, Phyllis developed a time log. A time log is a chart that measures how long it *really* takes you to finish a task. To use your time log, write a list of errands and tasks that routinely occur in your week. Write your estimate of how long you *think* each activity takes. Then, for a week, keep your log with you to record the start and finish time for each task. How long is your commute? How long does it take to drop off your child for soccer practice? How long does it take you to run errands on the way home from work? How long does meal preparation and clean-up take? Over the course of a week, a pattern will emerge showing you how long, on average, these activities really take you to do. With this information in hand, you can more accurately plan your schedule to accommodate the different tasks you have to do.

Get support in completing your time log. Let family members know about your project so that they can help remind you. Your child might enjoy being your official time keeper. Ask your time tutor to call or e-mail you daily to remind you to complete your time log. Even if it's not kept perfectly, you'll get a much more accurate idea of your *real* time expenditure. We've included a blank form you can duplicate.

Sample Time Log

Task	Start Time	Finish Time	Total Time to Complete	Comments
Drive to Music Class	3:20 p.m.	3:55 p.m.	35 minutes	Allow 15 minutes more drive time!

Time Log blank form

Task	Start Time	Finish Time	Total Time to Complete	Comments

Level Three Solutions:
Help from Professionals

Scheduling

A schedule is what helps your to-do list become a "done" list. A schedule is a when-to-do list that packages your tasks into small bundles of time, assigning a specific time for their completion. Scheduling your time does not mean you've abandoned all spontaneity. But scheduling is very helpful for those time periods when you need to function efficiently, because you have multiple tasks to accomplish. A schedule combines three elements:

■ your repeating daily time commitments;

■ less-frequent scheduled occasions and events; and

■ additional tasks that must be fit in around these existing commitments.

You'll need your PO or ADD coach to help you set up a schedule. A one-hour time-management session can help you prepare a schedule for up to three months, so it is a great investment. To make the best of your time management appointment, follow these steps:

1. Gather all your calendars, appointment books, day planners, time logs, invitations, flyers, notices, sticky notes, handwritten notes, refrigerator messages, and anything with a deadline or a due date on it. Your PO or coach will help you sort this out.

2. Inform your PO or coach about your staying power and your need for breaks.

3. Select only one calendar, day planner, or appointment book to use. Your PO or coach will help you with this.

Now your PO or coach is ready to help you marry your tasks to your time, a process known as scheduling.

Basic Scheduling

Basic scheduling includes accounting for your standing appointments; tasks that are time sensitive (that must be accomplished *by* a certain date, or must be accomplished *on* a certain date); and tasks that tend to recur daily, weekly, or monthly. That is what your PO or coach is looking for when she goes through your sticky notes, calendars, appointment books, to-do lists, scribbles on napkins, and so forth.

Standing appointments are blocked into your schedule first, then time to prepare for them is planned (scheduled). This is critical for people with ADD. If you have a dentist appointment, not much preparation is needed. But if you have a speaking engagement, part of scheduling includes blocking out time to prepare for the speech.

With your standing appointments and your preparation for them blocked in, you can turn to that massive list of one-time to-do items and tasks big and small. First, prioritize them. "First things first" is a great motto. A simple system of A, B, and C for prioritizing will work fine: A for top priority, B for next in priority, and Cs last. Block your As into your schedule, then your Bs and Cs. Your PO will also help you break down big tasks into smaller ones so that large tasks can be accomplished as a series of smaller ones.

It all sounds very neat and easy, but it's not always that way. With the help of a PO, coach, or time tutor, though, your scheduling skills will improve.

Eating Your Schedule

If scheduling in this basic, traditional way does not suit you, try "eating" your schedule, a more creative approach to scheduling. Eating your schedule involves dividing your tasks into "bites," "gobblers," or "munchers."

Bites

Bites are simple, single-step to-do's like an errand or a phone call that you can eat in one bite. Picking up Kelly's rented flute is an example.

Gobblers

Gobblers are to-do's that require concentration and gobble up more time than a bite. Usually a bite takes only minutes, while a gobbler, though it is a single task, can take hours. Paying bills and balancing the checkbook are examples of gobblers.

Munchers

Munchers are multistep, complex to-do's or mini-projects. A muncher is too big to gobble down at once, and is accomplished over a period of days or weeks. Reorganizing or remodeling your home are examples of munchers.

Your PO or ADD coach can help you sort your to-do's into bites, gobblers, and munchers. Here are some steps to take:

▮ Fold a single piece of paper into thirds.

▮ Title the left panel "Bites," the middle one "Gobblers," and the third panel "Munchers."

▮ List your bites (simple, single-step to-do's) on the bite panel.

▮ List gobblers (tasks that require more concentration and that will take hours rather than minutes) on the gobbler panel.

▮ List munchers (complex, multistep projects on the muncher panel.)

1. Now, place a star next to the most important bites, gobblers, and munchers—prioritizing them. If prioritizing is difficult for you (see Chapter 7), your PO or ADD coach can help.

2. Enter the starred bites, gobblers, and munchers into your schedule, assigning them to unscheduled times that fit around your existing time commitments and standing occasions.

3. After you've scheduled your starred bites, gobblers, and munchers, go back and schedule the unstarred ones. That way, you've made sure that you have time for your top-priority tasks before scheduling lower-priority ones.

Eat Your Schedule

Fold a sheet of paper into thirds, like a brochure.

Single-step, small tasks that take minutes

Large tasks that take hours

Complex, multistep tasks that take days

Bites

*Pick up cleaning

Call Dentist

Fax article

Mail taxes

Take clothes to thrift store

Gobblers

*Complete Taxes

Clean out hall closet

Buy interview suit

Write article

Munchers

Organize House

Organize Filing System

*Find Summer camp for kids

4. Scheduling munchers is more complicated than scheduling bites and gobblers. You'll need to work with your PO or ADD coach to break munchers down into doable steps. Essentially, a muncher is a series of bites and gobblers. Sometimes they must be done in a certain sequence; for example, if you're remodeling your kitchen, certain tasks must be scheduled before others. For other munchers, the sequence is more flexible, for example, if the task is to reorganize your home, you can choose to begin in any room.

Review

▪ ADD can affect your awareness of time.

▪ Use pattern planning.

▪ Block out unrealistic thinking.

▪ Don't bite off more than you can chew.

▪ Improve time sense by staying on task.

▪ Put a time tutor on your organizing team.

▪ Take green breaks.

▪ Reduce distractions to increase task completion.

▪ Develop worry outlets.

▪ Use a time log.

▪ Eat your schedule.

▪ Schedule your day according to mood.

▪ Work with a personal organizer to learn how to schedule.

Chapter Fourteen

Overcoming Overcommitment

Ted is a highly educated, intelligent person who also happens to have attention deficit disorder. Despite his ADD, he has managed to earn his Ph.D., although his dissertation took him several years longer than planned. He has been married for over twenty years, and has two daughters, both now in college. As Marian, his wife, has turned her attention away from their girls, she finds herself increasingly dissatisfied with her marriage. "I guess that I was so busy with our girls when they were growing up that I didn't notice Ted's patterns so much." Now, she frequently finds herself angry with Ted as he repeatedly arrives home later than planned. Not infrequently, he calls with an apology, saying that he won't be home until quite late due to some impending deadline.

Ted works for an educational think tank, where his job is to sit on committees, develop educational policy, write grant proposals, and participate in research projects. He finds the work fascinating and enjoys his interaction with other creative "idea people." The only problem is that his chronic overcommitment at work leads to greater and greater conflict at home. When he's up against a deadline at work, his immediate response is to cancel some commitment he'd made to his wife, assuring her that he'll make it up later. Because he tends to remain caught up in his work, he has little idea of how often he has let her down. In his mind it is "every once in a while, and only for a good reason." In her mind it is "most of the time. I can never count on him." Chronic overcommitment is beginning to seriously erode Ted's marriage. Marian's loud complaints are wake-up calls through which he is snoozing.

---

*

Karen's overcommitment has different sources. Like most women today, she is chronically stressed due to juggling both work and family commitments. Her ADD makes this juggling act even harder because she has difficulty developing organized, streamlined routines for herself and her family. The organizing challenges that so often accompany ADD lead her to forget to plan ahead. So, on top of an overly busy schedule, she's frequently pinch-hitting. Dinner plans go awry because she forgot to thaw the meat, or because she forgot that she had a dental appointment that afternoon.

> **Is this your story?**
>
> **It is if you:**
>
> ■ don't carefully consider your commitments before saying "yes";
>
> ■ have a hard time setting limits on your time; and
>
> ■ feel chronically overcommitted, but can't seem to find a way out.

To make matters more complicated, Karen is a single parent of two daughters, one in middle school and one in high school. After several very rough years following her separation and divorce, Karen and her daughters have pulled together, supporting each other as best they can, but Karen often feels that she has placed too many responsibilities on her girls because of the demands of her job.

Overcommitment and People-Pleasing

Karen learned to be a people-pleaser long ago as a way of compensating for her ADD foibles. She agrees to work late, whenever her boss asks, and agrees to take her daughters shopping in the evening, even if she's exhausted. Of course, the more she overcommits, the more forgetful and disorganized she becomes, triggering another round of compensating through overcommitment.

Overcommitment and Impulsivity

Overcommitment is a problem for many adults with ADD, especially those who tend toward the hyperactive end of the continuum. For some, it's as if life is a smorgasbord and their eyes are always bigger than their stomachs. Impulsivity leads them to dive in without carefully considering other commitments. Typically, they've crammed one more thing into their lives so many times that it's become their *modus operandum.*

High Cost of Overcommitment

If overcommitment is typical for you, you may even feel a sense of pride, at times, about the number of things you're involved in. As you rush from one activity to the next, you may not be aware of the cost, to yourself and to the people around you, of overcommitment. When you're up against the wall, struggling to meet a deadline, you quickly look for that individual that it is least costly to disappoint. Ted has fallen into a pattern of robbing his personal life to compensate for professional overcommitment.

For others, more often women with ADD, overcommitment results from approval seeking and difficulty in setting limits on the demands made by others. Karen lives with a frantic seesaw of imbalance—trying to measure on a daily basis whether she should shortchange her job to meet her daughters' needs, or whether she should disappoint her daughters to keep the boss happy.

You pay a high cost for overcommitment on a daily basis. You pay with a high stress level because you're habitually late. You pay with chronic fatigue because your overcommitment doesn't leave time for eight hours of restful sleep. Many people with ADD become almost proud of their ability to meet the crisis (often a crisis of their own creation) and prove the critics wrong. "I told you I'd get it done!" Sometimes adults with ADD become hooked on the excitement of crisis management as a lifestyle. For others, their overcommitment only leads to chronic anxiety because their life feels out of control and they can't find a way to keep a balance.

> **Overcommitment is the commitment of your time beyond its availability.**

The Out-of-Balance Life

When Ted runs out of time at work, he steals it from his relationship with Marian, from his family life, from his sleep, and from all of the other activities that are part of a healthy, balanced life. Sometimes an adult with ADD doesn't recognize the emotional cost of overcommitment until his family relationships are damaged beyond repair. For Karen, the greatest damage is done to herself. No matter what she chooses, she feels she's let someone down. Most often, she shortchanges herself, going without enough sleep, without time to relax or enjoy herself, as she tries to juggle the demands of work and home.

People with ADD tend to add complications and commitments to their life without subtracting old commitments to make room for the new ones. Reactively responding to the requests of others, or to your own impulse of the moment, typically leads to overcommitment. To lead a more balanced life, you must step back to take stock of the big picture, and then carefully decide what to add and what to subtract from your overcommitted schedule. Adults with ADD who remain in the reactive mode subtract things by default. When you try to keep too many balls in the air, you'll inevitably drop some. Instead of a planned decision, you drop a ball by accident—and often it's a high-priority commitment that is accidentally dropped.

Both Ted and Karen are guilty of "ADD math"—addition without subtraction. Ted continues to add commitments at work, stealing time from his personal life. Karen keeps adding commitments at home and at work, trying to "do it all," unable to recognize the limits of her time and energy.

Overcommitment

Level One Solutions:	*Understand What*
Ways to Help Yourself	*Drives Your Overcommitment*

Overcommitment has many sources. Sometimes the problem is related to poor time management skills, but often there are other psychological factors at work. You're not likely to learn to reduce your overcommitment until you understand all of the factors that influence you. Some common patterns are described below. Do any of these sound familiar? Do you:

- crave challenges and love finding a way to do the impossible?

- need high stimulation and like the thrill of fast-paced activities?

- like to be the hero who saves the day?

- find that you're unable to turn down an opportunity?

- get caught up in the enthusiasm of the moment?

- compulsively take care of everyone but yourself?

- take pride in getting more done than anyone else?

- tend to be a people pleaser who hates to disappoint?

If one or more of these patterns describes you, you'll need to find ways to meet your psychological needs that aren't so costly to yourself and to the people who are important in your life. Recognizing what's driving you is the first step toward changing your chronic overcommitment.

Executive Functions and Overcommitment

For some adults with ADD, the primary factor leading to overcommitment may be the executive function difficulties associated with ADD that cause poor self-monitoring and time management. For example, do you:

- realize you're in a time crunch only *after* you've made commitments?

- frequently rob yourself of sleep to meet your commitments?

- habitually underestimate how long a task will take?

- impulsively say "yes," before you've taken time to really consider the question?

- find that you're often pulled away from your task by a new interest or idea?

Habits to Counteract Overcommitment

If so, there are important habits you can learn to slow down your overcommitment merry-go-round.

Stop being a sleep thief

The idea of "enabling" developed in the addiction community. An "enabler" is someone who makes it easy for an individual to continue his destructive habit. You may be enabling your overcommitment if you're a chronic sleep thief. Karen fell into this pattern repeatedly. By trying to keep her boss happy and to meet her daughters' needs, she cheated herself, night after night. By robbing herself of sleep, she made it easier to continue her pattern of overcommitment. Finally, she learned to set a strict bedtime that allowed her to get seven to eight hours of sleep each night. Setting strict limits around the hours that she spent meeting her commitments helped her to become more realistic about what she could reasonably accomplish.

Become a better time estimator

Each day, as you list your to-do's, write down your estimate of how long each will take. Then keep track of how accurate your estimates are. Chances are great that you always underestimate. Keep working at your estimations each day until you're accurate in your estimates. Of course things will happen that are beyond your control. But becoming an accurate estimator of tasks within your control will greatly decrease overcommitment patterns.

Overcommitment

Put ideas in a cooler instead of on your plate

ADDers are notorious idea-generators. Often the generation and creation of ideas can lead to more and more work. It was Ted's idea to write a grant proposal for a manual on evaluating voucher programs. It was Ted's idea to join the State Office of Education's Committee for Non-Violent Schools. It was Ted's idea to award business people for their school mentorship programs. And aspects of all of these projects have landed on Ted's plate. Marian wonders how Ted got himself so involved in all of these projects. "Other people have ideas, but they don't all seem to be as overcommitted as Ted is," she observes. To Ted's way of thinking, if you have an idea and you don't act on it, it will vanish. He has no place to put them other than on his plate. "If I don't run with an idea, I forget it," Ted says.

But there are other places to put ideas than on your plate. One place is the "cooler," a place where ideas are stored. The cooler can be a drawer, a file folder, or an electronic file. One adult with an ADD sense of humor actually uses a cooler!

▌ Take a minute right now to identify a cooler for your ideas. Put a sign on the drawer, folder, or other container you have selected that says "Idea Cooler."

▌ As they occur to you, write your ideas on anything handy— slips of paper, sticky notes, or even napkins. It really doesn't matter.

▌ Every day, empty them into the cooler.

▌ Now get your calendar. On the thirtieth of every month write "Review Ideas." Review them more frequently if you need to, but always make an appointment with yourself; otherwise, you'll forget.

▌ Schedule times to act on an idea as your time becomes available through completion of earlier projects.

"Just having someplace to put my ideas has been a real plus. It helps me minimize my knee-jerk reaction to start working on every idea at once for fear I will forget the idea. Now the ideas never get lost," reports Ted.

Level Two Solutions:
Help from Friends and Family

Help from friends and family is in order when you've tried to make changes on your own but have been unsuccessful. When, try as you may, you fall into your old patterns repeatedly, it may be helpful to ask for help in setting limits and changing patterns.

Who Are You Kidding?

Do you continue to tell yourself the same old things? "This crunch is only temporary." "Next month, things will be back to normal." "This project was too exciting to pass up, but it will only last for a few months." And, do you keep believing yourself, despite so much evidence to the contrary?

When you receive messages from everyone close to you that you keep yourself in a state of overcommitment, you may need to assign someone as your time tutor to help you assess every new commitment—before you take it on. Your time tutor can help you keep your addition and subtraction in balance.

Saying "Yes" Without Overcommitting

For many adults with ADD, saying "yes" leads to trouble. There's already too much on their plate and each "yes" only makes their overcommitment worse. But with the help of a time tutor you can learn to say "yes" in ways that don't make your commitments careen out of control.

1. Learn to Say a Qualified "Yes"

Saying "yes" without thinking through the time implications is a classic way of becoming overcommitted. But you need not avoid saying "yes." You just need to use qualified ones. A qualified "yes" is enthusiastic and cooperative, but will not lead to overcommitment: "Yes, I'd love to, if I can turn over responsibility for my current project to someone else."

"Yes, I'm very interested, and as soon as my current commitments have ended, we can begin." "Yes, I'd be happy to become involved, but only on a consulting basis until I can clear out my calendar."

If you have trouble qualifying your "yes," work with your time tutor, even doing some role-playing, to develop the habit of the qualified yes.

2. The 1:2 Ratio Technique

For every new commitment you say "yes" to, say "no" to two old ones. Let's say Ted's colleagues want him to head up the annual awards dinner. Ted is a great choice. He's gregarious, enthusiastic, and knows all the people in the company. But Ted already has several committee involvements on his plate. He might say, "I'm interested, but I need a little time to think about it." Rule number one for keeping your enthusiasm from running amok is taking time to consider the consequences.

Then Ted, in consultation with his time tutor, chooses two existing commitments that can be retired in order to take on the new commitment. Ted is able to report back to his colleagues the next day. "If someone else takes over the education voucher programs, and the bulletins from the Office on Educational Reform, I'll head up the annual awards dinner."

Ted has proposed that he subtract two existing commitments (researching voucher programs and reading bulletins) in order to add one new commitment. Always retire *two* old commitments for every one new commitment you take on, because new commitments can swell to be larger than you anticipated and you don't want to find yourself overcommitted.

3. The Phase-In Technique

 Another way to handle overcommitment is to phase commitments in over time. Ted tells his colleagues, "I'm interested, but I need a little time to think it over." (Rule one: take time to consider.) Then, after consultation with his time tutor, he reports, "My plate is too full now. But in two months, when the voucher work is completed and the intern comes on to handle the state bulletins, I can join the committee or become chair."

Both of these "yes" techniques—the 1:2 ratio and the phase-in—buy you little breathing room. When you are asked to make a commitment, *always say*, "I'll need a little time to think about that." Then confer with your time tutor, ADD coach, or PO. Are there current commitments you can retire to bring the new one on? Can you phase in this new commitment? When you've established this with the help of your time tutor, you can report a "yes" back to the person asking you for a commitment. But it will be a new kind of "yes," a qualified "yes," the kind that does not lead to overcommitment.

Level Three Solutions:
Help from Professionals | *The Negotiation*

When you negotiate, you buy yourself valuable time to complete your work. You need not call it a "negotiation," but whenever you set up a compromise, you're negotiating. Your PO, therapist, or ADD coach are excellent people to practice negotiations with. All of them know how to role-play, have experience with negotiations, and will help you experience the negotiating process in a way that is as stress-free as possible.

Here is Karen's negotiating situation:

Karen's boss asks her to finish a report by Tuesday morning, but to do so she would have to work overtime (again).

First Karen plays the boss and the PO plays Karen. Then they reverse roles. This way Karen sees what its like on both sides of the table.

Boss: Karen, I need the report on my desk by Tuesday morning.

Karen: Tuesday would be difficult, but I can guarantee it by Thursday morning.

Boss: Thursday is too late.

Karen: Okay, I can have it for Wednesday by 5.

Boss: I'll need it earlier on Wednesday.

Karen: I can have it on your desk Wednesday morning, but that will delay the project I'm working on now.

Boss: That's alright. This report is top priority.

In the negotiating process, Karen's boss started out with Tuesday morning as the deadline—his inside position. Karen started out with Thursday morning—her outside position. But they ended up with Wednesday morning, a position somewhere in-between. Karen also negotiated letting another deadline slide, a critical technique in avoiding overload.

Negotiation Principles

▌ Always begin with a position that you expect to compromise.

▌ Never start where you hope to end—then there's no room for negotiation.

▌ Make the assumption that the other party expects to compromise too.

▌ Expect to meet somewhere between your starting point and theirs, although not always in the middle.

▌ Look for ways to meet their needs without overly compromising yours.

▌ Try to avoid expressing anger or antagonizing the other party.

▌ Let them know that you appreciate their situation, and communicate your position in a way that will elicit understanding.

▌ Look for ways to reframe the situation from win-lose to win-win.

Naturally, negotiations depend on the power and authority hierarchy of your business. In some cases, you won't be able to negotiate with your boss.

When Counseling or Psychotherapy Is in Order

When your overcommitment is long-standing, often there is more involved than the need for better time-management skills. If you've tried to implement several of the techniques suggested in this chapter and find that, even with the help of a time tutor or coach, your patterns of overcommitment continue, it's time to explore the psychological factors involved.

Some people with ADD can become addicted to overcommitment—the challenge and excitement of rushing to meet deadlines, of pulling off the impossible. Certain professions or jobs are magnets for individuals with high stimulation hunger. Jobs in the media, entertainment, and politics, or high-profile positions with attractive perks can become addictive and difficult to give up. ADDers with cutting-edge technical skills may be attracted to start-up companies where they work long hours for low pay with the dream of a big payoff just around the corner. Consciously or unconsciously, you may continue your overcommitment patterns because your behavior makes you feel important, needed, successful, appreciated, or stimulated.

When you're not able to modify your overcommitment patterns on your own, or when overcommitment is paired with other addictive patterns, psychotherapy can be very useful in helping you understand and change these patterns while still finding ways to satisfy your hunger for stimulation.

Overcommitment for many women with ADD is the result of a lifetime of trying to compensate for ADD traits, or trying to please others so that they can avoid negative reactions to ADD-related glitches. "So my boss won't be angry that I get to work late, I'll volunteer to work late when the office is in a crunch." A skilled therapist can help her work through self-esteem issues and help her to establish a more ADD-friendly lifestyle that can reduce her tendencies toward overcommitment.

Overcommitment

Review

- Understand your psychological need to overcommit.

- Problems with executive functioning can lead to an overcommitment.

- Say, "Let me think about it."

- Stop being a sleep thief.

- Become a better time estimator.

- Put ideas in a cooler instead of on your plate.

- Who are you kidding?

- Learn to say a qualified "yes."

- Practice the 1:2 ratio.

- Use the phase-in technique.

- Learn to negotiate.

- Sometimes psychotherapy or counseling is in order.

Chapter **Fifteen**

Plenty-of-Time Thinking

Steffie is a corporate trainer preparing to facilitate a training session. Since she has given this training several times before, Steffie believes it will only take a couple of hours to prepare. She'll need to go through a couple of boxes, pull out the relevant handouts, and copy them. Unfortunately, her week turns out to be extraordinarily busy and overcommitted. Day after day, those two hours she needs never seem to be available. Now it is the day before the training session. With a full day of work ahead of her, Steffie's only chance to prepare is in the evening, but she has an early-evening appointment she cannot change. "I'll just return to the office at 8:30, gather up what I need, and copy the handouts at the office," she thinks, pleased that her plan will still allow her a good night's sleep.

At 8:30, Steffie is exhausted. The effects of her stimulant medication have worn off. She cannot think clearly, so she drinks a cup of coffee. As she searches through her boxes of handouts, Steffie finds herself distracted, frequently stopping to read materials only marginally related to her training session. She has difficulty deciding among them. Then, to her dismay, she finds that her copy machine is out of order. So at close to midnight, it's off to the copy shop. Steffie has to do the copying

Is this your story?
It is if you:

- always think you "have plenty of time";

- can't estimate how long things will take to do; and

- fail to schedule specific times to complete specific tasks.

herself, since a clerk is unavailable. She arrives home at 1 A.M. feeling too wired to fall asleep easily and rises at 7:30 A.M. Her training session begins at 9 A.M., and she's already tired.

Fuzzy Time Budgets

If you tell yourself you have plenty of time, there's no need to be specific about how much time you really have. You're using a fuzzy time budget. You feel no need to decide which particular time you'll spend completing your task. There's so much time stretching ahead of you that you can afford to keep your schedule fuzzy.

It's like people who think they've got plenty of money in their checking account, only to find that they've run out of cash and have gone into overdraft. When you don't keep track of how you spend your time, however, there's no overdraft protection. Instead, to pay the bill, you must steal time from something else. In Steffie's case, she robbed herself of sleep. But even stealing time has its limits, and then the penalties start rolling in.

If not now, when?

Plenty-of-time thinking is related to the ADD tendency to live in the "now." Many adults with ADD tell themselves, "If it doesn't have to be done *now*, then I don't need to think about it *now*. I've got plenty of time."

Although there may be a great deal of time between *now* and your deadline, chances are that time is already committed to other things. It's a bit like thinking that you've got plenty of money because the checks you've written to pay bills haven't been subtracted from your bank balance yet.

Deduct committed time so it's not spent on other things

Your future time may still be "in the bank" but checks have already been written for future activities. If you don't block out specific hours from the "plenty of time" that seems to stretch endlessly into the future, it won't be there when you need it.

Evaluate the time needed for the task before you earmark a block of time

To earmark time for your task, you first need to evaluate how much time you'll need. If Steffie's handouts had been prepared, as she thought they were, her plan to make copies the day before her presentation wasn't bad. However, Steffie didn't evaluate the situation in advance, to make sure that her materials were ready. Only at the last minute did she realize how much work needed to be done.

Operating at Warp Speed

The ADD tendency to rush through things at the last minute may contribute to your inaccurate estimates of how long things really take. Often, when you're under the gun you can get things done in a hurry by operating at warp speed. Thus, you tend to underestimate the amount of time a task reasonably takes under normal conditions. You use warp-speed as your measure. Unfortunately, as you can see from Steffie's story, you are not always in top form. If you have ADD, your ability to function efficiently can vary widely. And even if you could, operating at warp speed causes high stress that contributes to a "crash and burn" pattern so common among adults with ADD in which they push themselves so hard at the last minute that they collapse, unable to keep up with daily responsibilities.

This Won't Take Long (I Wish)

A second factor in poor time estimating is wishful thinking. Many people with ADD don't like to admit the daily time cost of undesirable activities. You may not *like* that major portions of your day must be spent commuting, filing, completing forms, and so on. In your wishful thinking, you tell yourself that you can get to work in only twenty-five minutes (true, if there's no traffic), even though such thinking often makes you late to work. You tell yourself that you can get those handouts prepared in an hour or two (true, if you already have the handouts written and the copy machine is in good repair). Life often seems too tedious to those with ADD. So you plan your days as if you can use your teletransporter to fly above the rush hour and pretend that you can get all the boring stuff done "in a jiff."

Level One Solutions:
Ways to Help Yourself

Cushions

From a time-management point of view, plenty-of-time thinking can undermine even the best-planned day or week. So many things can happen that are unplanned—traffic, distractions, broken machines, lack of help, and the effects of medication, to name just a few that stymied Steffie. Even a well-organized person can get planning wrong when there is no cushion to allow for these unplanned circumstances. So the answer to the question of how long a task takes is: longer than you think.

Add a cushion to your thinking about how long things will take to account for the unplanned. People with ADD can underestimate tasks by as much as fifty percent. Here's the formula:

> **Your estimate of how long it will take**
>
> **+ fifty percent more time**
> _____
> **= *a better estimate***

The worst thing that can happen is you'll finish early and have more time to relax.

Watch Out

Analog watches and clocks, the kind that have actual faces and hands, can help you avoid plenty-of-time thinking better than your digital timepieces because you can graphically see the "distance" between one point of time and another. Steffie, when asked how long it will take her to do the photocopying, might have said, "Not long, maybe ten more minutes." But if she were to look at an analog watch, she could see that ten minutes actually takes up a pretty short distance from beginning to end and she might see that she needs more "distance" (that is, time).

Accurate awareness of time can also be promoted with the use of a special product called a Time Timer. As you set the timer, the length of time you've set is shown in red as a "slice" of the "pie" on the white clock face. The passage of time is clear at a glance because the red portion becomes increasingly smaller as the time goes by, becoming a sliver, and finally disappearing as the timer sounds.
Information on the Time Timer is available in the Resources section of this book.

Make Appointments with Yourself

A crucial step in time management that many people forget to take is to move items from a to-do list to the get-it-done phase by assigning a specific time on a specific day for performing each task.

Instead of thinking, "I need to work on that report this week," say to yourself, "I need to schedule three two-hour blocks of time this week to work on that report." Then go to your day planner and look for available time blocks. If they are not available, and if this report is a high priority, you may need to change other commitments. Once you've made an appointment with yourself to work on the report between two and four in the afternoon on Tuesday, you'll be more likely to protect this time from casual encroachments.

Balance Your Time-Bank Account

You've got "outstanding checks" in your time-bank account that you've probably never subtracted from your balance. When you "balance" your account—subtracting time for all your standard commitments and extra commitments, your "plenty of time thinking" will rapidly become more realistic. (See "pattern planning" in Chapter 13 for details about scheduling commitments to clearly see how much time is actually available.)

Anticipating Hyperfocus

When adults with ADD hyperfocus, they often lose all track of time, never coming up for air to check the time. When you don't have a clear sense of the passage of time, it can easily seem as if you have plenty of time to get other tasks completed. When you can anticipate your hyperfocus activities, then you can take precautions, such as completing other tasks first, so that hyperfocusing doesn't eat up all the time available. Or you can set an alarm to pull you out of hyperfocus so that you can move on to the next task.

Level Two Solutions:	Play the Time Guestimate Game
Help from Friends and Family	

 Use your time tutor to help you play a time game with yourself. With the help of your time tutor, write out the tasks that you must complete for the following day, with a time estimate beside them. Your time tutor may want to venture a time "guestimate" alongside yours so that you can see who is more accurate. Your list might look like this:

Drive to work	35 minutes
Download and respond to e-mails	30 minutes
Write letter regarding . . .	30 minutes
Team meeting	60 minutes
Lunch	60 minutes
Respond to voicemail messages	45 minutes
Work on quarterly report	90 minutes
Consult with George on project	30 minutes
Pick up dry cleaning	15 minutes
Groceries	25 minutes
Pick up kids at day care	15 minutes
Drive home	15 minutes

Then, the next day, write down the actual time that you spent engaged in these tasks. You'll find that unexpected things happened—more traffic than usual in the morning, more e-mails to respond to, a need to consult with someone before writing the letter, or your meeting with George dragged on for nearly an hour.

See how accurate or inaccurate you were. Was your time tutor more accurate? Now, play the game the next day. Do you find that you're leaving more time for the unexpected? That you build in more time for the usual?

Keep playing this game, on a daily basis, with the help of your time tutor, until you find that you're pretty accurate in your estimates. You can consider that you've had a great day if most of your estimates are correct, even if a traffic tie-up in the evening extends your commute by twenty minutes. You can't control everything. But when you find that you're full of excuses about why things took longer, you need to face facts and allow for contingencies.

Level Three Solutions: Help from Professionals

If plenty-of-time thinking is chronic and causing you constant, stressful lateness and you can't turn it around with the methods discussed in this chapter, consider discussing it with your ADD therapist or coach. You may need to develop strategies, specific to your own situation, to combat these patterns. An ADD expert can help you pinpoint the particular patterns that lead to your last-minute rushes and can help you problem-solve to correct these recurring patterns. The added structure and support of a coach or therapist will make your time management strategies more likely to succeed.

Review

- Beware of fuzzy time budgets.
- You can't always operate at warp speed.
- This won't take long (I wish).
- Build in time cushions.
- Use analog clocks and watches.
- Use a Time Timer.
- Make appointments with yourself.
- Balance your time-bank account.
- Anticipate hyperfocus.
- Play the Time Guestimate game with your time tutor.
- Work with your therapist, to pinpoint problems and develop strategies.

Chapter **Sixteen**

The State of Rushness

Alisa lives in the state of rushness. She's always rushing from one event to the next, and is often late no matter how much she rushes. Her children have become so resigned to her pattern of lateness that they are accustomed to her screaming demands to "Get in the car!" followed by the breakneck drive to school, school supplies left behind, rapid good-bye kisses among flying lunch boxes and bookbags.

Alisa knows that she needs gas in the car. Throughout the day, she mentally reminds herself to get gas so she won't have to stop in the morning and add precious moments onto what will no doubt be another rushed morning. But she never remembers at a time that's convenient. As so often happens, she forgets, and finds herself pumping gas in the cold morning, kicking herself for not finding time the day before.

When she's in the state of rushness, nothing can happen fast enough for Alisa. Even an average traffic light causes her to drum her fingers impatiently on the driving wheel, and curse under her breath. Slow drivers frustrate her. Whizzing past them has resulted in several speeding tickets. Every unpredictable small event that slows her progress makes her nearly explode.

As she arrives at work, she dashes into the building late (again), pushing the elevator button repeatedly, though she knows full well this does not speed up the elevator. "I've just got to get my act together," Alisa declares to herself, shaking her head in frustration over the stress she feels as she begins her workday.

Alisa's rushness doesn't end when she gets to the office. In fact, most of her weekdays are spent in a continual state of rushness. She enters her office late and then makes a frantic effort to complete the memo that must be ready for her ten o'clock staff meeting. As usual, it's done at the last minute and Alisa hands it to the administrative assistant to make copies as she rushes down the hall at five minutes after ten. And so her day goes.

Low Frustration Tolerance

Many adults with ADD have low frustration tolerance. It's part of the general emotional reactivity that is common among those at the hyperactive/impulsive end of the ADD continuum. Frustration may also be a reflection of high stress levels and anxiety. A domino effect can occur in adults with ADD: poor planning, forgetfulness, tension, anxiety, and low frustration tolerance cause an emotional tinder box in which the next thing—it could be almost anything—can trigger an emotional explosion. Everyone has such an experience occasionally, when, after repeated frustrations, a "last straw" causes overreaction. Some adults with ADD, especially those who live in a state of rushness, are operating in emotional overload much of the time. For Alisa, chronic anxiety plus poor time management leads to lateness and a sense of urgency that escalates her frustration level every morning.

Some adults with ADD have a generally low tolerance for frustration. For some, the brain's emotional center, the limbic system, is hyperaroused much of the time, with the chronic stress of ADD contributing to that arousal. As a result, minor frustrations can seem intolerable.

| Level One Solutions: |
| Ways to Help Yourself |

If your days resemble Alisa's, it is critical that you find ways to reduce the levels of stress and frustration in your daily life.

In-Between Times

Unforeseen circumstances are a source of frustration for many people—those small events, out of our control, that seem to plague us just when we most need to be on time or to arrive prepared. The best way to reduce the frustration of unforeseen circumstances is to anticipate them and make time for them. Some disasters are beyond prediction or control. If you must make a trip to the emergency room with a family member who is critically ill, or if you are involved in an automobile accident on your way, no one will fault you for lateness. However, when you are repeatedly late because of predictable "unforeseen" events— those that should be expected because they're so frequent—you need to adjust your timing.

To allow for these very regular unforeseen events, it's important to build in "in-between" time to your schedule. Alisa has no in-between times. She butts one activity right up against the next and runs her appointments back-to-back. Even a tiny bit of running behind on one activity compounds the problem. Ten minutes late leaving the house becomes fifteen minutes due to slow drivers which becomes twenty-five minutes when she stops for gas.

Alisa cannot predict which unforeseen circumstances will arise, but many small events are "predictably unpredictable" such as:

∎ adverse traffic conditions;

∎ the needs of a hungry child or one who has to go to the bathroom;

∎ putting gas in the car;

- last-minute phone calls that have to be taken before you can leave the house; and

- a forgotten item that delays your departure as you retrieve it.

Allowing for time in-between events can lower your frustration level considerably.

Does "One-More-Thing-Itis" Contribute to Your Rushness?

Alisa has a bad case of one-more-thing-itis—the sudden impulse to do one more thing before she walks out the door. Sometimes the phone rings and she cannot resist answering it. At other times, she does one more thing because a task has not occurred to her until she is preparing to leave. Only then does she think to check whether there is enough water in the dog's bowl or whether she's locked the back door or whether she has the directions she needs to get to her destination.

The best solution is a "departure checklist." Just as a pilot has a checklist that he carefully goes through before takeoff, Alisa needs a departure checklist outlining the steps she needs to take before leaving the house.

Departure Checklist

Make your departure checklist bold and bright. Hang it in a conspicuous spot that you'll pass on your way out of the house.

- Find keys, cell phone, day planner, and eyeglasses—put them in pocket or purse.

- Pack briefcase with files or paperwork.

- Check calendar and to-do list.

- Gather all items needed for appointments and errands (directions, receipts, items to return, etc.).

- Turn off stove, TV.

■ Lock doors, turn on alarm.

■ Stop, think. Did I forget anything?

■ Hear the phone ringing? That's what answering machines are for.

■ Suddenly remember something? Write it down and do it later!

Develop the habit of gathering all listed items ahead of time (the night before) and placing them on your "launching pad" (see Chapter 4 for more on launching pads).

Plan to Arrive Early

Plan to arrive at your destination fifteen minutes *early*. If you are usually late, this goal may seem impossible, but it's not. Your habitual lateness usually results from cutting it close, and allowing no time for departure preparation. When you leave no room for error, and combine this with forgetfulness, not to mention traffic tie-ups, you're sure to run late and to spend your day feeling stressed.

Two key steps to arrive early:

1. Build in fifteen extra minutes for departure preparation. This is the time to go through your departure checklist, *not* a time to engage in one-more-thing-itis.

2. Plan to *leave* fifteen minutes early.

In combination, this means a half-hour shift in your departure preparations. The rewards are *immediate:* you won't leave feeling stressed, you won't drive frantically or yell at the traffic in frustration. And, if all goes smoothly, you'll have time to decompress at the other end before launching into the next activity of your day.

Don't Drive Yourself Crazy

An important part of developing an ADD-friendly approach to life is the acceptance that sometimes your ADD will get the best of your well-laid plans. There will occasionally be times when you're running late. The trick is to not compound your troubles by becoming frustrated.

The number-one traffic violation is speeding. The number-one reason for speeding, according to police statistics, is "I'm late." Instead of risking life and limb, develop strategies to lower your stress level. Being late isn't the end of the world, but having an accident because you're speeding could be. Practice deep breathing to calm yourself when you're running late. Play soothing music, or listen to the radio. Instead of berating yourself, give yourself a break, and then do some constructive thinking about ways to avoid the problem next time.

Smooth Departures

Alisa began to realize that one of the sources of her lateness came from a lack of departure preparation. She made a list of events that had made her late in recent weeks, and developed a plan of action.

- Set a morning departure time fifteen minutes earlier.

- Check the gas level on the way home each evening and stop to fill up the tank.

- Develop a schedule for routine car maintenance so that breakdowns are unlikely.

- Stock the car with an extra key and money for tolls.

Alisa's sixteen-year-old daughter, Tina, is learning to drive. Alisa has brought her into the departure preparations. It is Tina's responsibility to make sure that no car is blocking her mother's car in the driveway each morning. On cold mornings, Tina goes outside early, starts the car to warm it, and scrapes any ice off the windows in preparation for departure. In exchange, Tina is allowed to drive the car in the morning, dropping her brother off at middle school, then heading to her high school, where her mother takes the wheel, driving herself to work.

Avoid Procrastination Propulsion

Many ADDers increase their motivation for unappealing tasks by putting things off until they become urgent—using procrastination propulsion to get going. Although this may work, it is a high-stress way to live, leading to anxiety, loss of sleep, and disorganization in other areas as you have to "drop everything" to respond to the self-created "emergency." Alisa's procrastination is a major factor in the rushness of her workday. She has difficulty completing paperwork and writing memos, typically doing them at the last minute, and sometimes not even then. Her dynamic energy and marketing skills lead her boss to overlook much of her lateness, but the chronic stress takes a huge toll on Alisa and certainly impacts her relationships with the family when she arrives home feeling tired and irritated.

Now that Alisa has developed strategies for a smoother morning departure, she's turning her attention to the causes of rushness throughout her day. Alisa doesn't have a perfect record yet, but she's focused on leaving fewer things to the last minute.

Constructive Waiting

Waiting, even for half a minute, used to raise Alisa's blood pressure. In her state of rushness she was always stressed, pressured by the next activity for which she was typically late. Now, Alisa has learned to wait constructively. To her surprise, she even looks forward to a few unexpected minutes when someone keeps her waiting. She gets many things accomplished while she waits by always carrying a "wait pack" with her filled with reading material or note cards to send. In good weather, she takes advantage of waiting times by getting in a brief walk—clearing her mind and getting exercise at the same time.

Relaxation Techniques to Reduce the Effects of Stress

Numerous strategies have been listed above to reduce the number of frustrations in your daily life that lead to chronic stress. Some stress is inevitable, and some frustrations are beyond your control. When you're in a frustrating situation it's critical that you learn ways to lower your stress response. In fact, recent studies have demonstrated that chronic stress can have corrosive effects on mental and physical health.

Deep breathing

Breathing in a very deep, slow, controlled manner, inhaling through your mouth and exhaling through your nose—is an activity that you can engage in unobtrusively, and can be done in your car if traffic is your source of frustration.

Muscle relaxation

These techniques are easily done in many situations and can go a long way toward counteracting the effects of stress. Stress leads to muscle tension, especially in the neck and shoulder areas. Tensing and releasing these muscle groups rhythmically can help reduce muscle tension. Another good muscle relaxation exercise is shrugging. Bring your shoulders up toward your ears, hold them as high as you can for thirty seconds, then release. Repeat several times to reduce stress in the neck and shoulders.

Level Two Solutions:
Help from Friends and Family

Good Timing Gets Things Done

One of the reasons that Alisa has lived in a state of rushness is that she leaves tasks undone that repeatedly result in mini-crises because she must rush to complete them at the last minute. In talking with her time tutor, Alisa has begun to analyze her procrastination patterns. One of the common reasons that she avoids certain tasks is that she tries to fit them into the times of day when she's most tired. For example, she tries to wrap up her paperwork at the end of each day. Alisa greatly dislikes paperwork and resents that so much detailed record-keeping is required by her company. By four-thirty in the afternoon, she's tired and eager to leave the office, so she tends to rush through paperwork, rarely completing it. The same pattern is true for doing errands on the way home. When Alisa is on her commute home, she'll only stop for absolute necessities, such as purchasing groceries for dinner. Otherwise, she'd rather not stop, so she passes by the bank and the gas station, telling herself, "I'll do it tomorrow."

Strategic Scheduling

At the suggestion of her time tutor, she now rarely schedules paperwork or errands at the end of the day. Instead, she starts her day with paperwork. A fresh cup of coffee and a high energy level can propel her quickly through these frustrating details, freeing her to concentrate on the more important tasks of the day. She no longer plans to run errands on the way home. Now, Alisa schedules errands on her lunch break—with the added benefit that she gets out of the office for half an hour. Other errands are scheduled for Saturdays and Sundays, when she is less rushed.

Problem-Solve with Your Time Tutor

Make a short list of three main items that represent your "Why I Have to Rush" list. Go over it with your time tutor (or PO) and devise an anti-rush strategy for every item on your list.

- The kids never wake on time.
- The kids are never ready to go when I am.
- I'm always hunting for something I need at the last minute.
- I need to stop for cash or gas.
- I'm not prepared for a meeting or appointment and have to rush at the last minute to gather materials I need.
- I never leave enough time to get from point A to point B.
- I usually underestimate how long things will take.

Develop time-management strategies

Alisa, with Marsha, her time tutor, went over her list. "Marsha is a great time manager. We went over my list of what makes me late and worked out a little preparedness plan for each problem area." Time-management problems are often intertwined.

Alisa has listed many factors that contribute to her state of rushness: lack of planning, disorganization, procrastination, and inaccurate time estimation. If you're like Alisa, and find yourself frequently living in a state of rushness, there are suggestions in other chapters of this book that may be directly useful. First, with your time tutor, you need to analyze the source of the problem. For example, if you're rushed in the morning because of frantic searches for misplaced items, creating a family "launching pad" will greatly decrease your morning rushness (see Chapter 4). If poor time estimation is a major factor, try to improve your sense of time by keeping a time log (see Chapter 14).

Prepare the Kids for Departure

In Alisa's case, as is true for many people with ADD, a big part of the morning rush is related to the children not having a good morning routine. Below are some suggestions of ways to help your children develop a smoother morning routine.

If the kids are not prepared to leave the house when Alisa is ready to go, the stage is set for confrontation and frustration. Just as Alisa and her time tutor analyzed the sources of her rushness, they also analyzed what leads to morning chaos and confusion for her children. With her time tutor's help, the family devised the following changes.

- *Earlier bedtime.* Alisa's kids are tired and hard to rouse in the morning. Her time tutor strongly suggested an earlier bedtime for everyone in the family. Rested kids wake up more readily.

- *Two alarm clocks.* To wake her kids, Alisa uses two alarm clocks *and no snooze alarm.* She sets the first alarm to go off near the child, and sets the second clock to go off three minutes later across the room so the child has to get out of bed to turn it off. That wakes them and keeps them awake.

- *Rewards for being ready on time.* Until Alisa's children develop new habits, they need a big motivation to change. Alisa came up with the idea of breakfast treats. Any child who's at the breakfast table by 7 A.M., having completed *all* of their get-ready-in-the-morning tasks, gets a special breakfast treat, while dawdlers get a grab-and-go breakfast to eat in the car.

(For more suggestions on streamlining your children's morning routines, see Chapter 4.)

Attention-Grabbers for Kids

ADD kids wait until the last minute just like adults do. Decals, stickers, and signs are attention-grabbing to kids and make them attend to things sooner rather than later. Alisa's kids always wait until she is practically in the car to feed the cat. She made a trail of contact-paper footprint decals on the floor. The first footprint decal the kids step on when they get out of bed says "Brush your teeth, sleepy head." On the kids' bathroom floor another decal reads "Did you wash your hands?" Another one, leading to the kitchen reads "The cat is hungry." Try not to make decals that give orders, like "Feed the cat," "Wash your hands," and so on. Just try to be encouraging so they attend to things in a timely manner.

Level Three Solutions: Help from Professionals

ADD Coaching to Reduce Rushness

Alisa has done a great deal of problem-solving with her time tutor. She was fortunate to have a friend like Martha on her team. If working with your time tutor isn't effective, or if you feel you need more structure and support to change your rushness habits, try working with an ADD coach. Reducing rushness requires changing many different habits— which is never easy. A coach can help you problem-solve and prioritize so that you can be successful in changing habits. One of the big mistakes that many adults with ADD make is to try to change too much at once. When they're unsuccessful they become discouraged and quickly return to their old habits of rushness.

With a coach, you can build habits gradually, so that each habit lends support to the next. Regular phone contact with your coach can keep you on track and can help you problem-solve when snags arise.

When Your Anger Is More than a Sign of Stress

Alisa was very concerned about how short-tempered she had become with her children, particularly in the morning as they were running late. She had scared herself more than once as she took chances in traffic trying to make up for lost time. As she gained better control of her time and her schedule, Alisa's frustration level decreased, her driving habits improved, and family relationships became calmer.

For Alisa, stress was the culprit that led to her angry explosions. Other factors, however, are often the source of anger. If you find that practicing better time management and stress management doesn't solve the problem, it's a good idea to consult a therapist. Anger and irritability are often signs of unrecognized depression that may need to be treated with psychotherapy and/or medication.

Ask for a "Reasonable Accommodation" at Work

Someone who is expert in working with adults with ADD can help you to understand your rights under the Americans with Disabilities Act, and can offer advice on requesting a "reasonable accommodation." It's important to understand, however, that asking for accommodations, without showing your employer a positive attitude and a strong work ethic, is not likely to meet with success.

Alisa's boss is aware of her ADD. They are exploring a more flexible schedule that would permit Alisa to work on a flex-time schedule. In this way, when Alisa's best efforts to leave the house on time fail, her stress level doesn't have to go into the stratosphere. So long as she works 40 hours each week, her boss is satisfied.

If you need advice on what your accommodation rights are and how to invoke them, reach an ADD organization listed in the Resource section of this book, and speak in private with the human resources director of your company. Also talk to your therapist. Disclosing your ADD is not always the best course of action. You'll need to carefully weigh the benefits and costs of doing so.

Participate in "Time-Out" Activities

The demands of highly structured work schedules are difficult for everyone, and especially difficult for those with ADD, who must expend much greater effort to keep track of time. To relieve the stress of being "on time all the time," time-out activities can be highly therapeutic for adults with ADD. Time-out activities are those in which you can engage fully, feeling "outside of time," temporarily suspending the relentless pressure to keep track of time. Drs. John Ratey and Ned Hallowell write:

> We also see people with ADD hyperfocusing on an activity, like rock-climbing, or driving, or work, probably because it allows them to forget about the expectations associated with "time." Our patients frequently report that they are most calm when completely caught up in the thrill of it all, whatever that "all" may be. It could be fun, a catastrophe, or a life-or-death crisis. These situations allow the ADD person not only to get into forward motion, but also to forget, to disregard that they need brakes in the first place. In an emergency, it's full speed ahead. What a relief. (p. 283)

Your ADD coach or therapist can help you decide which time-out activities to engage in. Vacations (real ones, without a lot of scheduled, planned activities) are great. Thrilling (but not dangerous) physical activity, such as hiking up a mountain trail, or doing something new and exciting (and safe) can inject stimulation into your regular life and provide an out-of-timeness that nourishes your ADD soul. For others, the greatest relief comes from truly having a day off, a day in which they can wander from one activity to another without any pressure to attend to the needs of others, or to be in a certain place at a specific time.

Seek Careers That Are More Time-flexible

Many adults with ADD choose to work for themselves so that they can set their own highly flexible time patterns, limiting the number of weekly events that must occur at specific times. Others seek jobs that accommodate their night-owl tendencies, eliminating the ADD struggle with early-morning rising to prepare for the day. Speak with your ADD coach or therapist for more ideas about choosing a career that is a better match for your struggles with time.

Anxiety

Anxiety is a very common coexisting condition for many adults with ADD, and especially for women with ADD. Your "state of rushness" not only adds to anxiety, but can also be the result of chronic anxiety and stress. You may need to consult a therapist and consider medication for anxiety as well if anxiety plays a strong role in chronic stress and "rushness."

Review

- Chronic stress and low frustration tolerance are results of being rushed all the time.

- Schedule in-between times.

- Try not to succumb to one-more-thing-itis.

- Make a departure checklist.

- Plan to leave early.

- Don't drive yourself crazy.

- Prepare for departure.

- Procrastination propulsion is not a good long-term solution to lateness.

- Wait constructively.

- Use relaxation techniques to reduce the effects of stress.

- Good timing gets things done.

- Problem-solve with your time tutor.

- Reduce the rushness for kids.

- ADD coaching can reduce rushness.

- Consider therapy: anger can be a sign of more than stress.

Part *Five*

Paper Organizing

Chapter **Seventeen**

Fear of Filing

"**F**ile it? But if I file it, I'll never find it!" This is Martha's response to a suggestion from a well-meaning friend that she put some of her piles of papers away in a filing cabinet. Martha is a very successful businesswoman. Recently her fifteen-year-old daughter was diagnosed with ADD, and she and her daughter have read and learned as much as they can about it. Though Martha herself has not been diagnosed, she feels certain her disorganization problems are neurologically based.

"I just can't explain it any other way," Martha says. "No one I know in business has a desk like mine. Most days I can't even see the top of my desk. If I don't keep the papers out in front of me, I forget what I'm supposed to do about the papers. Everything falls through the cracks. The paper clutter is really affecting my business. I can't bring clients to my office because it's such a wreck. And even though I know where everything is, it takes me longer and longer to find what I'm looking for. I need a secretary, but I could never hire one because nobody knows where anything is but me."

Out of Sight, Out of Mind

Martha, like Edgar in Chapter 8, is an OosOom, a person for whom out of sight is out of mind; however, Martha's biggest struggle is related to her paperwork. Unless Martha has her papers right out in front of her she forgets

where they are and what needs to be done with them. Martha fears, and rightfully so, that if the papers on her desk were to disappear (that is, be filed) she would not remember to deal with them. Bills would go unpaid. Projects in progress would be neglected. The visual reminders to take action would be wiped out, and instead Martha would have to depend on her memory. Furthermore, Martha fears that if her papers were filed, she'd never remember where to find them.

Level One Solutions:
Ways to Help Yourself

Keeping Papers in View

Martha has the right idea. She functions best when she can *see* what she needs to do. But her way of keeping things in view, by piling things all over her desktop and credenza is a very inefficient method. To keep things in view, remember:

Horizontal = Hidden
Vertical = Visual

A stack of papers is a visual cue, but the more stacks you have and the higher they are, the more time it will take you to find what you're looking for. Because stacks are horizontal, only the uppermost piece of paper is revealed and everything below is concealed, making it difficult

Fear of Filing

to find things. Also, since you are the only one who knows where anything is, secretaries, administrative assistants, or a family member will find it very frustrating trying to find something in the event that you are not around. Eventually, you will also run out of space. And then there is the way your space looks with papers everywhere. Such a cluttered environment will eventually annoy even the most understanding coworker or spouse.

Keeping things in view, but arranging your files vertically, will provide better visual cues and will allow you to find papers faster. Vertical filing systems include:

Vertical Organizers

Courtesy of Eldon.

Courtesy of Eldon.

▌ vertical file holders;

▌ filing crates on casters; and

▌ vertical desktop filers.

Unlike stacks, which can tend to homogenize your papers into one disorganized mass, papers held vertically can be separated, identified, and labeled by using file folders in a step-up holder. The file-folder tabs are clearly revealed, showing a subject, title, or other identifier.

Use Color

Use colored file folders instead of manila file folders. Colored file folders are very visually appealing and engender action-oriented responses in us. Use traffic light colors as your cues: green files mean completed and ready to go, yellow files warn you to get ready to do something, while red files mean urgent. Other colors can allow you to "code" papers by type. All financial papers might be in blue files, for example, or all client files in purple. When files are color coded, you can find them more readily. And if a yellow file is misfiled it stands out and can be quickly retrieved, keeping your files more organized.

X-ray Vision

It would be wonderful to have X-ray vision and be able to see through file folders and other containers right to the contents inside. The closest thing to having X-ray vision is to use transparent file folders. They are made of plastic and come in a wide range of see-through colors. Buy removable adhesive labels so you can label the file folders.

The Hot Spot

The hot spot is a place on your desk or table, or wherever you do paperwork, that contains a red, see-through plastic sleeve or red transparent file folder. It must be red because red is identified with urgency. The hot spot contains a maximum of six pieces of paper representing action that must be taken before the day is out. It may include a few key phone calls to make, an item to discuss with a coworker or family member, or something essential to fax or e-mail today. It may even be a note to yourself. A hot spot works like a stubby to-do list (see Chapter 8). Just as your stubby to-do list should contain only a few items, those that *must* be done today, your hot spot folder should contain no more than six pieces of paper. Too many items and your hot spot becomes just a pile of papers to process. More than six pieces tends to corrupt the integrity of the hot spot.

Chunky Papers

Chunky papers are bulky reports, bound materials, and thick bunches of related papers. Chunky papers need different containers than the files you use for skinny papers. Clear off the bulky clutter on your desktop by using:

Chunky Paper Organizers

Courtesy of Fellowes Manufacturing Co.

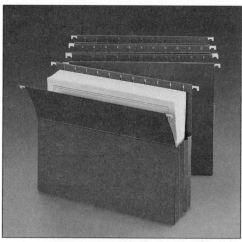

Courtesy of Smead Manufacturing Co.

- box bottom file folders;
- magazine holders; and
- binders.

Box-bottom file folders can accommodate up to three inches of paper. They will not fit inside a desktop holder, but you can easily arrange box-bottom files like books on your desk or credenza. They can also hang inside a filing crate or a filing cabinet. Chunky papers can also be organized by using magazine holders. Another organizing solution for chunky papers is binders. Three-ring binders can hold chunky papers from one-half to five inches thick depending on the kind you buy. You will have to three-hole-punch the paper, but once you do, the binders can sit neatly on a bookshelf getting a lot of paper off your desk. Be sure to label all box-bottom files, magazine holders, and binders so that you can see in an instant what is where.

"Verb" Your Papers

Verbs are action-oriented and when used on files and papers they suggest what *to do* with your papers rather than what they are called. Verbs identify actions to take. Nouns, such as titles, subjects, and categories, identify what the papers are, but not what to do with them. "Verbing" your papers gets you ready to take action on them. Many people with ADD are kinesthetic, or action-oriented, so they can relate

Verb Your Papers

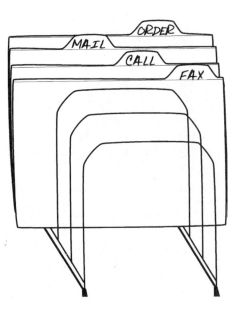

more easily to verbed or action-focused sorting. Verbing your papers also takes a step out of the decision-making process: when you pick up a verbed paper, you've already decided what needs to be done with it.

Set up a series of file folders vertically on your desk with verbs on their labels. Common verbs to use on file labels include: "Fax," "Order," "Subscribe," "Copy," "E-mail," "Call," "Pay," and "Reply." Now, go through your most active papers and file them by these verbs. This encourages action and groups your papers together by like action. You are more apt to take action if your papers are organized by verbs. And the more actions you take, the fewer papers you have.

Grouping papers by action is very efficient. Instead of jumping from a call to a fax to an e-mail, you are more apt to do a clump of calls in one sitting, a bunch of faxes at one time, and several e-mails in a row, accomplishing these tasks more quickly. This is a better use of your time.

When you're verbing your papers, be sure to put urgent papers in the hot spot.

Bag Your Papers!

You don't have to use file folders for your papers. Anything transparent will do. For example, one woman puts all her papers into individual two-quart plastic food storage bags. There is a space to write on each bag, indicating the contents and a place for a date that she

Fear of Filing

uses to note when the papers were first placed inside. She hangs the food storage bags on clip-style skirt hangers and hangs the whole "filing system" over a door.

Paperweights

Paperweights are another way to differentiate one stack from another. Martha has a small, heavy marble owl paperweight on top of a stack of papers she needs to read for professional development. "The owl is a symbol of wisdom, and if I ever read all this stuff, I hope to be wiser," Martha says. A lion or weasel or other animal paperweight might represent papers from your boss. One client of mine has a piece of a railroad tie on a stack of her papers. Her family line includes many train conductors and engineers. The railroad tie reminds her of her family, so underneath the railroad tie paperweight is a stack of papers related to her genealogy research.

Level Two Solutions:	Put a Paper
Help from Friends and Family	**Partner on Your Organizing Team**

 A paper partner is a friend or family member who is good at organizing documents, files, and papers. A paper partner knows how to put something away and retrieve it again and is good at creating simple categories. Your paper partner can help you in your office or home office or even just around the house wherever paper accumulates. Use your paper partner to help you put the following solutions in place.

Get Rid of Your Filing Cabinets!

Martha retired her filing cabinets for storing active files because they tended to hide her papers from her. "I called my filing cabinets a black hole. Once I put something in them, I could never find it again." Instead, she has moved the contents of her filing cabinets into plastic crates, like old-fashioned milk crates, on casters, holding vertical hanging files. With this new storage system, each folder is easy to see and retrieve. Your paper partner can help you convert your filing cabinets to crates on casters and set up color-coded hanging files. An added benefit: the crates are mobile. Martha can scoot a crate over to the phone, roll it near the computer, or even roll it out of view into the closet.

Using Filing Cabinets for Long-Term Storage

Rolling Filing Crate

Courtesy of Esselte.

Although Martha has learned that rolling crates are better for storing active files that she needs to access frequently, there is a role for filing cabinets. They are great for storing:

- inactive materials you need to keep for some reason;

- materials you save for very occasional reference; and

- archival materials like back taxes that have to be kept for a long period of time.

Create an Index

So that you don't forget what you've filed away in your filing cabinets, create an index of their contents.

A simple index of the filing cabinet's contents (what files are in which drawer) will help you counteract the "black hole" effect. Arrange the contents of your filing cabinet alphabetically. Then simply list the contents alphabetically by drawer. Now you have an index of all the files in the filing cabinet and which drawer they're in.

An index is even more important for your crate filing system because you'll be in and out of it more often. But the process is the same. Arrange the contents alphabetically and list them in your index. A computerized index is more convenient as it can be updated easily, allowing you to print out a new clean copy, whereas a handwritten index will become messy as you add or delete items.

Ticklers

A tickler is a kind of notebook that lies flat on your desk. It has pages numbered one through thirty-one on tabs up the side, referring to the days of the month. Papers, notes, or entire file folders are placed behind the date on which action should be taken for those items. Each morning, the folder "tickles" you to check today's page for any items behind it. For instance, Martha could slip a note behind the thirteenth that says "Finish the Jones report." Then, on the thirteenth, she checks behind the tickler page number 13 and finds her note, reminding her to finish the Jones report. Because the tickler is her visual cue, she no longer needs to keep papers in sight, and can file them in her active files until action is required. Because many papers do not have dues dates or deadlines, you'll have to set dates yourself depending on how long it will take you to process that paper or finish the task.

Everyday File Fast Sorter

Courtesy of Cardinal Brands.

Shopping for Paper Organizing Tools

Shopping in large discount office stores, which offer the best prices, can be very overwhelming. The choices are vast, the shelves are endless, and it may be tempting to just walk in, turn around, and walk out. Take along your paper partner or a friend. Or shop instead in a small but well-stocked stationary store. Or consider ordering from a catalog. Some companies offer free next-day delivery for orders over $20.00.

Level Three Solutions:
Help from Professionals

Off-Load Your Desktop

If you have ADD, it is likely that you use stacks and piles to remind you of actions to take. But there are other devices that you can use to remind you of actions to take besides the actual, physical stacked papers themselves. These off-loading devices combine paper management with time management and task management. They allow you take the paper on your desk and put it away (paper management), but permit you to remember to complete the task it represents (task management) by a certain deadline (time management). A PO can help you off-load your desktop without losing track of your schedule or to-do's.

Examples of off-loading devices are:

▮ handwritten to-do lists;

▮ day-planner entries; and

▮ ticklers.

Martha needs to finish the Jones report. She writes this on her to-do list. But she also writes it on a specific day in her day planner. Now she can file away (paper management) all the papers related to the Jones report because the to-do entry (task management) stands in for the actual papers. And the entry on her day planner alerts her to when she must do the report (time management). Your PO can help you to list all the tasks that might now be represented by papers piled on your desk and then enter them in your day planner or other time-management system.

"Mutter" Your Papers

The "muttering" filing system promotes organizing your papers emotionally, instead of categorically. It works by tapping into your emotional response to your papers. For instance, have you ever picked up a piece of paper and said, "I better hold on to that. It might come back to haunt me"? The muttering filing system would have you file that paper in a folder called "This will come back to haunt me." Your PO can help you set up a muttering filing system.

Muttering System

Courtesy of Squall Press.

WHY CAN'T I FIND THIS WHEN I NEED IT!

DID I GET PAID FOR THIS YET?

I CAN'T BELIEVE I HAVEN'T WRITTEN BACK YET!

I HAVE GOT TO CALL THESE PEOPLE!!

Setting up a Muttering Filing System

1. Supply your PO with straight-cut tab folders (the kind with the tab that runs the entire length of the file folder instead of one-third cut) and a thin black marker.

2. Walk through your office and pick up one loose piece of paper at a time.

3. Mutter out loud the first thing that comes to your mind.

4. Have your PO write that "mutter" on the file folder and place the paper inside.

5. Do this with all your loose papers.

6. Arrange the folders vertically on your desk.

Popular mutterings include:

▐ "This may come back to haunt me";

▐ "If I win the lottery";

▐ "This makes me feel good";

▐ "Good ideas";

▐ "These prove my point";

- "Treasures";

- "This is funny stuff";

- "For Uncle Sam";

- "Why can't I find this when I need it";

- "Did I get paid for this yet?";

- "I can't believe I haven't written back yet"; and

- "I have got to call these people!"

Review

- Work in conjunction with your out-of-sight, out-of-mind (OosOom) nature

- Remember that Vertical = Visible, and Horizontal = Hidden.

- Use color coding for easy retrieval.

- Use transparent containers for visibility.

- Create a hot spot on your desk.

- Organize chunky papers differently than skinny papers.

- "Verb" your papers.

- Don't file active files in filing cabinets.

- Use filing cabinets for long-term storage.

- Create an index.

- Use a tickler.

- Off-load your desktop.

- Use the "muttering" filing system.

Chapter **Eighteen**

Backlog Blues

Elliot, a computer programmer, and his wife, Dotty, a real estate agent, both work at home. Their papers are *everywhere,* leaving barely any room to move about their office. Every surface of their home—every table, chair, countertop, shelf, window sill, wherever a piece of paper can land, contains magazines, newspapers, loose papers, faxes, clippings, catalogs, junk mail, maps, you name it. The guest bedroom, long abandoned, now serves as a storage room for boxes of old tax forms, older newspapers and magazines, and loose papers of unknown origin.

Elliot has a wide range of interests, and a lot of half-finished projects lying around. He's researching buying a new computer, and upgrading his website. He and Dotty are active campers and like to stay up-to-date on the latest equipment and places to camp. They subscribe to dozens of magazines and newsletters, and order from several catalogs. "We also plan to renovate the house for the new baby and pay more attention to our financial investments, so more paper is on the way!" Elliot says jokingly.

"We've always lived like this," Dotty said. "Elliot is a packrat and though I don't save papers like he does, it just doesn't bother me much. I'm out of the house much of the time, busy with my own clients, and we're not big on entertaining. Most of the stuff is dead, inactive stuff. We're on top of the bills and important papers like that. But now that Elliot's business is taking off, and we'll be starting a family, we thought we'd better try to organize this stuff."

Much of the way we learn, get informed, and stay up-to-date is paper-driven. Whether it's magazines about our favorite sports, newsletters with investment advice, or correspondence with our bank, paper, more than other media, continues to dominate. Based on our interests, we gather papers, keep them while they are interesting and useful to us, and then, when our interests change, most of us shed the papers we have accumulated because they are now less interesting and less useful. As we move from job to job, home to home or interest to interest, ideally the flow of paper in our lives follows a process of gather-keep-discard, gather-keep-discard, based on our new needs and interests. This keeps us from becoming backlogged with a glut of unnecessary papers.

Is this your story?
It is if you:

- maintain a disorganized backlog of accumulated papers;

- collect materials related to a wide range of interests; and

- tend to keep a lot of reading and reference materials.

> **The ideal paper flow should be a continual process of Gather – Keep – Discard**

Certain ADD patterns can distort or interrupt the discard portion of this process. These include:

- difficulty with decision-making;

- a pattern of ignoring routine life-maintenance activities;

- a wide range of interests pursued with enthusiasm, but rapidly dropped;

Information Overflow

- a difficulty with project completion;.

- a dependence upon paper as a visual reminder; and

- an unrealistic sense of what you'll actually have time to read.

These patterns have been discussed earlier in relation to clutter management and time management. This chapter will address how these ADD patterns contribute to paper backlog. Your wide range of interests brings more paper into your home, and your difficulty with decision-making keeps the papers there. To discard requires a decision. Typically, the ADD default decision is "I'd better keep it. I might need it." An unrealistic sense of time leads you to delude yourself that "someday" you'll read all those magazines and catalogs. To compound the paper problem, a tendency to leave projects incomplete leads you to save all the books, catalogs, and papers that relate to each project. To throw the papers away is to admit you'll never finish the project. And, finally, you may hang on to paper as a memory aid.

Level One Solutions:
Ways to Help Yourself
Gathering Guidelines

Use the following guidelines to reduce the amount of papers you gather. If you find them helpful, you may want to laminate a printed list of guidelines and post it in a visible spot in your office, where you open the mail, or other places where you tend to gather papers.

Gathering Guideline Questions

1. *Am I still interested in knowing/doing/having this?* (Elliot was once keenly interested in martini bars, but this interest has waned since he married.)

2. *Do I know/understand this already?* (Elliot is now a pro at Internet shopping. He no longer needs a magazine article for beginners.)

3. *Is a better/fresher version of this likely to come into*

my life soon? (Elliot is tempted to keep an article on hot mutual funds, but did you know that financial information becomes obsolete eight minutes after it comes off the press?!)

4. **If I will use/read/do/share this, will I do it before it goes out of date?** *(Elliot plans to buy an SUV in a year or two, but the information he has will be out of date by then. It will make more sense for him to gather SUV information when he's closer to his purchase date.)*

5. *Can I deal with any regret I might have if I throw it away?* (Elliot knows that even if he makes a mistake and throws something away that he should not have discarded, he might regret it, but he'll get over it.)

Read Your Reading Materials

The best solution for handling a backlog of reading materials is to read them! This may seem obvious, but unless you read your material it has nowhere to go and stays in the "gather" phase. Once read, it can move to "keep" (in your filing system) or "discard." Left in the "gather" mode, reading materials can only accumulate, cluttering your workspace as well as the rest of your environment. Finding the time to read, especially professional reading, needs to move into the mainstream of your activities (see Chapter 7 on prioritizing): if reading material piles up, it's clear that reading during random unplanned moments isn't working. You'll need to develop a plan to keep up with your non-recreational reading.

■ Separate recreational reading material from professional reading.

■ Read whatever you can, whenever you can. (See Chapter 16 on constructive waiting.) Keep reading materials in the car, your briefcase, the office, house, and other convenient places.

■ Set up regular reading times for professional reading. Fifteen minutes a day, an hour and fifteen minutes a week, and five hours a month are equivalent. Choose the regularity that suits your needs and pattern plan your reading time. (see Chapter 13 on pattern planning.)

▌ Protect your reading time, giving it the same high priority that you would give a meeting with your boss.

▌ Learn how to skim.

▌ Be selective. The monthly newsletters of each professional organization to which you belong may not be of equal importance or value.

Choosing What to Read and How to Read It

Guard your reading time carefully, selecting only the most important or interesting material.

Materials that Deserve Careful, Detailed Reading

▌ A legal contract such as a business agreement, real estate contract, will, financial agreement, or other legal document.

▌ New information on areas of professional interest.

▌ Books or articles related to current areas of interest.

Materials to Skim

▌ Professional newsletters.

▌ Advertisements (ads solicited for comparison shopping would move to the careful reading category).

▌ Newspaper articles, unless of particular interest.

▌ Magazine articles, unless of particular interest.

▌ Catalogs, unless you are immediately considering a purchase.

Deciding whether to read, skim, or discard

1. Read the first two sentences of the first paragraph.

2. Read the first sentence of the second paragraph.

3. Read the first sentence of the last paragraph.

This will give you enough information to know if the article entertains, interests, amuses, informs, or educates you. If it does none of these things, discard it. If you decide to read it, but cannot read it now, flag it with a sticky note or pull it out of the periodical altogether. Toss it in your reading box.

How to Skim

Skimming involves a level of effort somewhere between the brief glances that allow you to decide whether to read it at all and the detailed, word-for-word reading that should be reserved for only the most important material.

Skimming professional material

It's often helpful to skim a document with a yellow highlighter in hand to highlight an important point or two.

1. Read the entire first and second paragraphs.

2. Read the opening sentence of each succeeding paragraph, choosing to read the entire paragraph if the opening sentence is eye-catching.

3. Highlight a few important facts or phrases.

4. Read the entire last paragraph.

Skimming recreational reading material

Few newspaper or magazine articles warrant close, careful reading.

Information Overflow

1. Read the first paragraph.

2. Glance at photos and hit the highlights—some, but not every paragraph's opening sentence.

3. Read the last paragraph.

Go on an Information Diet

One effective way to reduce your paper backlog is to reduce the amount of incoming reading material. The amount of information that we are bombarded with daily can be overwhelming. When you're an adult with ADD with a long list of interests, you may experience more information overload than most. The solution? Go on an information diet.

- Cancel your daily newspaper. If you find that you often don't read your daily paper, or that time spent reading it would be better spent on other things, you should consider receiving a Sunday newspaper only. A Sunday newspaper, supplemented by a weekly news magazine, radio reports, and television news shows may be more than sufficient to keep you up-to-date.

- Cancel redundant magazine subscriptions. Do you really need both *Time* and *Newsweek?*

- Drop yourself from newsletter and e-mail listserves you don't have time to read.

- When a newspaper arrives, yank out the sections you read and throw away those you don't.

- Choose the Internet for your source of selective information, the radio for local news, the TV for national news, and do away with newspapers altogether.

- Be selective, not reactive. Advertisers rely on reactivity—hoping that if it comes into your home you'll reactively read it.

Are You an Information Junkie?

Adults with ADD tend to find many ways to escape from the tedium of daily life-management tasks. While you may not feel you can justify spending large amounts of time on activities that are clearly recreational, you may fiercely defend reading the newspaper and watching television news shows as "valuable" activities.

Being an informed person is essential in a democratic society, but those with ADD may expand this civic duty until it has qualities of escapism, even addiction. If you find that you spend hours on the couch watching news shows, or read the paper from cover to cover on a daily basis, it's important to ask yourself whether this has become a task-avoidance technique. Instead of mowing the lawn, doing the laundry or dishes, or running errands, you're spending time that you can ill afford "informing" yourself.

Level Two Solutions:
Help from Friends and Family

Barbara Hemphill, in her book *Taming the Paper Tiger* notes that "in many cases, the real issue with 'To Read' papers is not to read, but to remember" (p. 129). Remembering what you have so you can use it when you need it is a key issue for adults with ADD. That is why so much backlogged, accumulated paper finds its way into reading stacks. They are not really reading stacks, but remembering stacks. "I put my directory of HMO providers in my reading stack, not because I am going to read the directory, but so I can remember I have it when I need to find a health care provider," notes Elliot.

The Reminder Filing System

This filing system is your temporary set of reminders and is meant only for dated material containing information that you need at your fingertips. It is not meant for professional material or for long-term storage of important papers.

Information Overflow

219

The reminder filing system and index takes time to initially set up, so often it's best to create the system with the help of your paper partner. Once it is set up, it is very easy to use.

■ Hang twenty-six hanging files inside a filing crate.

■ Insert the letters A through Z into the tabs, one letter for each hanging file.

■ File all your papers alphabetically.

■ Don't label your files with any categories or subcategories.

You don't even need file folders! Simply put the papers right down into the hanging files.

Elliot has clipped articles on campsites that have facilities for young children. He writes "Camp Sites—Children" on the top of the article and files it in the C hanging file. ADD goes in the A hanging file, HMO directory under H, investments information in I, Ritalin in R, and so forth.

"I was worried I might not remember that HMO was filed under H. I thought I might forget and check under M for medical or D for doctor." That's where a simple index comes in.

A simple index will remind you where you have filed things. To make an index:

■ Purchase a small, half-inch thick three-ring binder.

■ Inside, place a set of alphabetized tabbed three-hole-punched dividers.

■ Use each divider as your index for that letter, writing a list of papers filed under that letter and adding to the list as you add papers during the year.

■ Once a year—the beginning of the calendar year makes an easy-to-remember marker—purge your files, crossing items off your index as you purge them.

Keep your notebook index in a separate hanging file at the front of your file crate.

Hire a Clipper

If you make a list of your interests, you can hire someone to clip your newspaper, magazine, and newsletter articles of interest to you and you can remove yourself from the process entirely. Naturally, nobody is as good a clipper as you are, but when you weigh the time it takes skim, clip, and file against the 5 percent of articles your clipper might miss, it's a bargain. Great clippers include:

■ high school and college students;

■ interns; and

■ volunteers.

One woman hired the teenage girl next door as her clipper. She collects her magazines, newsletters, and periodicals, giving them to her clipper on a weekly basis; along with her list of interests. In exchange for clipping the articles, once a week, the woman gives the teenager a ride to and from the mall. Your own children can be groomed as clippers too.

Focus Your Interests

Focus your attention on what's most important to you, clearing out old interests to make room for the new. To get focused and make room for the future, try this exercise with your paper partner.

How Wide *Are* Your Interests?

1. Grab a stack of miscellaneous papers.

2. Stand in the middle of the room, leaving plenty of floor space around you.

3. Imagine three concentric rings around your feet: One ring near your feet, the next ring about two feet farther out, and a third ring four or five feet away.

4. Place a large trash container next to you.

5. Look at the first paper in your hand. If it concerns a highly valued interest of yours, put it down on the floor in the inner circle. If it is of less interest to you, put it in the second ring. If you want to save it but it really only interests you slightly, put it in the third ring.

6. Toss all the papers, one at a time, into one of the rings. Just make quick, intuitive decisions about the papers. The longer you ponder the harder it will be. If a piece of paper no longer interests you, throw it away in the trash container.

7. If you come across a paper related to financial, medical, business, or professional matters, set it aside to sort according to methods described in Chapter 17.

How Wide Are Your Interests?

When you are finished, you will be surrounded by your papers arranged according to your level of interest. Save the papers in the innermost ring in your reminder filing system. Commit to saving the best articles, the most informative columns, and the latest information only on these topics.

Second-ring papers are the ones most apt to grow, so be very choosy about these broader interests. Make sure you are not just saving them out of habit. Then file these in your reminder filing system.

Consider letting go of your third-ring interests altogether.

Rotate Your Interests

The sorting system described above may be difficult for some adults with ADD, especially for those who have difficulty prioritizing. In the exercise above, if you find that you're putting most papers in your innermost ring and almost nothing in your outermost ring, you're having difficulty prioritizing. Everything seems important to you, and you're resisting giving anything up.

If this is your experience, then try rotating your interests instead. Sorting by rotation may help you set some of your interests aside for now, so that you can focus on a few interests. By rotating your interests, you keep them all, but rotate them in and out of action.

Use the ring method

To rotate your interests, use the same ring method, but label the rings "now," "later," and "next year."

Set a strict limit on the number of interests that can be placed in the "now" ring, as well as in the "later" ring. If you have difficulty setting limits, get help from your time tutor.

Once your papers have been sorted into "now," "later," and "next year," place the "next year" papers in storage boxes, loosely grouped by category. File the other papers in two rolling crates labeled "now," and "later." Then create an index for each crate, just like the index described in the preceding exercise.

During the year, you are free to move any interest you choose from your "later" file to your "now" file, so long as you move an equal number of interests from "now" to "later." You are also free to add an interest to your "now" file that hasn't been there before. The only rule you should follow is to keep a limit on the number of interests in your "now" file, moving the rest to "later."

Once a year, bring out your "next year" storage boxes. Decide whether you want to rotate any of those interests into your "now" or "later" files. Remember, as you rotate an interest in, you must rotate another interest out into the "next year" file boxes.

Level Three Solutions:
Help from Professionals

The Body Double

 For many with ADD, dealing with paper piles can trigger such feelings of overwhelm, even anxiety, that they cannot stick with it long enough to create order. If this is true for you, a body double may be your answer. A body double is a passive partner who sits quietly by your side while you sort through your papers, handing you papers one at a time. Although your body double does not organize or even offer you advice, his role is very important.

A body double creates an atmosphere in which organizing can take place. With a body double present, you are able to remain focused on organizing and not be distracted by other things. In this way, the body double acts as a kind of anchor, anchoring you to your organizing activity.

Working with a body double

▪ The ideal body double is quiet and unobtrusive. You may have a friend or family member who can fill this role, but often a PO is best.

▪ Put two chairs side-by-side at a desk or table.

▪ Pull a trash container nearby.

▪ Put a stack of papers on your body double's lap.

▪ Have your body double hand you papers one at a time.

▮ Toss papers that are no longer needed in the trash.

▮ "Verb" all papers that require action (see Chapter 17) and place them in the appropriate action files on your desk.

▮ Continue until all the papers on your body double's lap have been processed.

▮ Take a break.

▮ Then do another stack if you (and your body double) have the time and energy.

The Crew

The crew is another option for organizing a large quantity of accumulated, mainly inactive papers. You are a member of the crew, along with one or two assistants, supervised by a professional organizer. Together, you and your PO assemble the crew. Assistants can be friends or family members. The crew presorts large quantities of papers according to categories established by you and your PO. After all papers have been presorted, then you and your PO sort through each category of papers, eliminating, filing, or setting them aside for action, as appropriate. Using a crew:

▮ reduces overwhelm;

▮ makes a large job go faster;

▮ keeps up morale;

▮ keeps you focused; and

▮ gives you a sense of progress as space is rapidly cleared out.

Paper Tiger Software

If you are computer literate you may want to use software to help you organize your papers. The Paper Tiger enables you to file and retrieve computer files, hard-copy documents, books, CDs, anything that you collect by using keywords. When you create a file on the software, you enter keywords about that file and its location in your office. Then, whenever you need to find that file again, you type in any of its keywords, and in five seconds the computer tells you where to find the file. You can print out indexes of all your documents and can cross-reference files. Check out www.papertiger.com for more information.

Create!

If you are an adult with ADD with strong creative interests, then consider organizing your papers by creating something with them. Consider whether the materials you are gathering are the makings of a book, an album, a presentation, or a class curriculum. Creating a product from the information you are gathering is one way to organize it. It packages the information and leaves you free to move on to other projects. If you undertake a creative project, an ADD coach is a good choice for seeing you through the steps. They can help you plan out the project, stay on task, and see it to conclusion.

Review

- Observe the gather-keep-discard cycle.
- Use gathering guidelines.
- Read your reading materials.
- Choose what to read and how to read it.
- Learn to skim.
- Go on an information diet.
- Put a paper partner on your organizing team.
- Use the reminder filing system.
- Hire a clipper.
- Focus your interests.
- Rotate your interests.
- Use a body double.
- Hire a crew.
- Try the Paper Tiger software.
- Create something from your papers.

Chapter **Nineteen**

Paper Money

Dan has three active checkbooks, all from the same account. He simply grabs the one in view, since trying to find the most current one amid the mound of documents on his desk would be an all-day affair. "I haven't balanced my checking account in over a year," Dan says. "It's a good thing I have a healthy balance and overdraft protection." Going through his financial papers, Dan and his PO counted nine check registers, seven checkbooks from five accounts, and four years' worth of bank statements. He also has five credit cards, three trust funds for grandchildren, and several retirement accounts. "I'm up to my ears in statements! I'm always paying extra late fees, and no matter how much I try, I can't find a bill-paying system that I can stick with. I'm behind on my taxes. Every time I sit down to reconcile a statement or review my finances, I get overwhelmed or feel bored. I can feel my eyes glazing over, so I abandon the effort. Thank God I have a good income or we'd be in financial ruin."

Dan recalls that his mother and father always argued about money— well, not money really, but the paper that represents money. "My dad had financial papers all over the house, just like me." Dan's son and grandson have ADD and from what he has read, Dan might have ADD too.

The negative impact of poor financial management is cushioned for Dan by his high financial bracket. However, few adults with ADD enjoy such protection from their ADD challenges. Mary's situation is more typical. A single woman in her early thirties, Mary has been seriously in debt since college. She's never managed to pay her student loans consistently, and has been burdened with penalties and interest for the past ten years. Little planning has gone into her financial decisions. For example, she purchased a new car recently, telling herself that she was making a good financial decision. The car was moderately priced in comparison to the luxury cars that some of her peers had purchased. "And besides, I won't have to worry about repair expenses with a new car," Mary reasoned. A few months later, Mary's roommate became engaged and moved out of their two-bedroom apartment. Mary had known her roommate since college days and had been comfortable sharing living space with her. Now, she was reluctant to advertise for a new roommate. She couldn't imagine living with a stranger.

> ## Is this your story?
> ### It is if you:
>
> ■ find keeping track of financial papers particularly troublesome;
>
> ■ tend to make impulse purchases;
>
> ■ are financially overextended; and
>
> ■ often pay taxes or bills late.

Saddled with a new car payment and now facing a doubled rent payment, Mary's finances went into free fall. Overdue notices from charge card companies and her student loan office were rolling in. She couldn't even manage to make minimum payments on all of them.

Financial Paperwork—an ADD-Unfriendly Activity

Financial paperwork calls on many areas of weakness for adults with ADD. Organizing papers, filing them where they belong, making careful notations, and filling out forms are activities that are typically difficult and frustrating for adults with ADD. Adults with ADD often react with impatience to paperwork or record keeping. Financial paperwork is ADD-unfriendly for several reasons:

- It's detailed—and many adults with ADD are prone to overlook details in their rush to complete an unappealing, anxiety-provoking task.

- It requires consistency—another ADD challenge. You may carefully record every check in your financial software program for a month, but typically your system falls apart as you become focused on other activities and forget to maintain the system.

- It is a multistep process—another ADD challenge. Multistep tasks are often difficult because forgetfulness and distractibility combine to throw you off track somewhere in the process. Writing the checks, and addressing and stamping the envelopes, won't do you any good if you stash them in your briefcase and forget to mail them for days.

ADD and Financial Anxiety

While Dan is somewhat cavalier about his financial mismanagement, most adults with ADD cannot afford his relaxed attitude. Mary, like many other adults with ADD, lives with chronic anxiety related to poor money management. Good financial management requires record keeping, planning, and self-control. Due to impulsive purchases and disorganized record keeping, many adults with ADD are seriously in debt. The response to indebtedness is often a combination of juggling and denial. "I don't know how much I owe. I'm probably afraid to add it all up," Mary remarks to her PO.

Doing financial paperwork forces you to add it all up. Unpaid bills, overdue notices, bank statements that you're unable to balance, and tax forms that require records you've not carefully filed away can all trigger anxiety that leads to avoidance of financial paperwork. And so the cycle continues. As you avoid financial paperwork, more problems develop, leading to more anxiety, leading to more avoidance.

Managing investments can be another source of anxiety. Good investment strategies require consistency, planning, decision-making, and record keeping. Checking out hot stocks on the Internet can be exciting for many with ADD. But when those hot stocks take a nose dive in value, the ADD reaction may be to quit tracking investments altogether, to avoid the anxiety of watching your investment account balance plummet.

Math Anxiety and Financial Paperwork

Financial documents draw meaning not from words, but from numbers. It is numbers, not words, that are their text. Numbers have a way of arraying themselves on a printed page in a manner that can seem confusing to the eye and the mind to organize. Dan's experience is quite common. Many adults with ADD have never been good at keeping track of the details of their life, and numbers are nothing if not exquisite detail. Combine anxiety with impatience (both common ADD traits) and you have an adult who typically glances at financial forms, tosses them in a pile, and relies on the bank, the IRS, or the credit card company to send them a loud, urgent message before they feel compelled to respond.

Level One Solutions: Ways to Help Yourself
Reducing Anxiety and Paperwork Avoidance

There are a number of strategies to reduce your anxiety and increase your accuracy when you work on financial papers.

Pick a time when you're at your best

Handling financial paperwork requires extra concentration and effort, so the first important step is to tackle your financial paperwork when you're at your best, not when you're rushed, tired, or frustrated after a long day.

Choose a quiet, nondistracting setting

Dan knows he will need to concentrate hard on his financial papers, so he has learned to work on his financial papers under quiet conditions. He prefers a small, almost closed-in space, so he has set up his bill-paying center on a small desk in the corner of his study. He only uses this work space for financial papers and keeps the desk surface cleared off so that he can concentrate without distractions. Dan is amazed at how much better he can concentrate and how much calmer he feels than when he tried to balance his checkbook amid his other paperwork clutter.

Self-talk

Self-talk can be helpful when dealing with financial matters. Dan now says out loud, "Okay. This is a complex financial statement. I have to concentrate to decode it. Running away won't help. I can do this."

Dan's struggle is simply his desire to escape the frustration and tedium of financial paperwork. Mary's self-talk takes on a different quality. Not only are numbers and record-keeping difficult for Mary, but she is filled with anxiety as she faces the dreaded bottom line each month.

Mary has learned to reassure herself and to congratulate herself on tackling this difficult task. She tells herself, "I should be proud of myself for taking this on instead of running away. I can't solve all of my financial problems overnight, but if I stick to my plan, I'll get there."

The Envelope Bill-Paying System

If you are not computer oriented, you can manage your bills with a bill-paying kit that keeps all the things for paying bills in one place. Once you set up your kit, you'll find that bill paying is smoother and more streamlined. Set the kit up and keep it in the same place all the time.

Bill-Paying Kit

Bill-Paying Kit

▌ Four large manila envelopes labeled:

  ▪ "Bills to be paid by the 10th";

  ▪ "Bills to be paid by the 25th";

  ▪ "Charge card receipts"; and

  ▪ "Paid" (you'll need a new "Paid" envelope each month).
  Write the month on the envelope also.

▌ Stamps

▌ Return address labels

▌ Blank envelopes

▌ A calculator

▌ Pens or pencils

▌ A trash basket

▌ A clear plastic food storage bag to contain all small kit items.

▌ A nice basket with a handle for easy toting that is large enough to hold all kit items.

Stow the kit right where you will be paying your bills and put the wastebasket nearby. When you receive a bill, keep only the bill and the return envelope. Toss any offers, notices, or other papers that come with the bill. On your day planner, write a reminder on the tenth and twenty-fifth days of each month to "pay bills."

Bill-Paying System

On the tenth or twenty-fifth of each month, take out your kit.

1. Pull out last month's bills from the "Paid" envelope.

2. Check the balance of the current bill to make sure that last month's payment was credited to you before you write this month's check.

3. Write the check—noting your account number on the check to ensure that your payment will be properly credited.

4. Enter the payment in your check register.

5. Enter the payment amount on the bill.

6. Write the check number on the bill receipt.

7. File the receipt in this month's "Paid" envelope.

8. Return last month's paid bills to last month's "Paid" envelope.

9. Put a stamp on the return envelope, and put the check and return statement inside, making sure that the address shows in the envelope window.

10. Put stamped envelopes on top of your briefcase or purse for mailing.

To streamline your bill paying, copy the list above, laminate it, and keep it in your bill-paying kit so that it's handy as you pay bills every two weeks.

Electronic Bill Paying

Your bills can be paid on the Internet, reducing most of your financial paperwork. Internet bill paying, offered by most banks, allows you to direct your bills directly to the bank or bill-paying service. The service notifies you by e-mail of each bill that comes due, but doesn't pay it without your permission. You are provided with regular e-mail statements documenting the payments. They'll even maintain your electronic checkbook and finances. No paper, no stamps, no checkbook! You have to like technology—and trust it—to use such services. If you're ready, try www.paymybills.com or ask about electronic bill paying at your bank.

> → **Reduce the number of bills you must pay by using one credit card for all purchases, including gas and groceries. Pay it off each month. Your bill paying will be quicker, and you'll have an automatic record of your expenditures.**

Take Advantage of Technology

If you are computer literate, financial software can definitely improve the organizing of your financial records and papers. The computer was originally designed for computing financial data. It's what the computer is best at. Financial software programs can allow you to retire your checkbook altogether and greatly simplify your financial bookkeeping. Financial software allows you to keep an electronic checkbook, print out checks for each payment, automatically balance your checking account, track all your payments in every category imaginable, and generate reports. Look into financial software packages at your local computer store.

Organizing Your Checking Account

If you choose the non-computerized route of using a checking account, *use only one checkbook.* Keep it in your purse or briefcase. Develop the habit of using it and returning it to its home.

Make sure it has a distinctive cover, like a geometric design or a color other than dark blue, so that it's easy to see if it is away from "home." Keep several emergency checks with a check register in another location in case the checkbook disappears altogether.

Lost checkbooks

If you lose your main checkbook, stop writing checks and look for it. If you cannot find it, use an emergency check until you find the checkbook. If you are unable to find your checkbook, purchase another one, start with a fresh pad of checks—the next set in your check sequence—and note at the beginning of a new check register that previous checks have been lost. If your old checkbook emerges at some later date, keep the check register for your records, but destroy unused checks to eliminate confusion in the check sequence. *Never* keep more than one checkbook in use.

Check registers and record keeping

Use the type of checks that automatically create a carbon copy of your check—that way, you'll always have a record of the check. Use two lines to enter items on your check register. It will be easier to enter, read, and track the entry.

Capture your bank receipts

Capture loose deposit slips, withdrawal slips, and ATM receipts in a large manila envelope hung on the wall. Label it "Banking." Keep last month's bank statement inside and throw in a pen and a small calculator.

Balancing your account

When you receive your checking statement each month, grab everything out of the envelope (and any deposit, withdrawal, and ATM receipts that might still be in your car, pocketbook, and briefcase). Take out your checkbook and balance it, either on paper or using a financial software program.

If you are unable to balance your account, and cannot find your calculation error, most banks will provide the service of helping you to reconcile your account. This service may entail a fee, but is well worth it to keep your records straight.

Organizing Other Accounts

Dan assembled a series of green three-ring binders (green stands for money) on a shelf. Each binder represents a separate investment, retirement, or fund account. The statements he receives from each account are already hole-punched, ready to insert. He just pops them into the right binder when they arrive. Then, prior to meeting with his financial planner, he reviews the statements.

The binders will keep a lot of bulk out of your filing system and keep the statements handy. Be sure to label the spines. After you receive your year-end statements, you can throw the monthly or quarterly binder contents away and replace them with the year-end statement. Relabel the spine for the new year. Use binders with internal pockets in the front and rear covers so you can also stow important literature from the financial institution regarding that account right in the binder.

Plastic Money

The more plastic you use (charge cards and credit cards), the more paper you will have. Credit card companies will inundate you with paper receipts, offers, statements, and information. The fewer cards you have, the better. Select one card with the lowest interest rate possible. Use low-rate credit cards in place of department store and gas cards, whose rates are typically higher.

Credit card offers are scheduled to come to your home at least every six weeks. If you are not in the market for a new credit card, toss the offers you receive out unopened. If you are in the market for a new credit card, collect the ones with the best introductory offers and put them in the bill-paying envelope marked "Pay by the 25th." Consider the offers then. There is no need to consider credit card offers more frequently than once a month.

If you shift credit card balances to cards with low introductory offers, be sure to clearly mark on your calendar a date several weeks prior to the end of the low introductory rate. Charge cards count on you to forget about the rate change, and you may find that you're paying a much higher rate a few months from now.

Receipts

There are only four financial reasons to keep a receipt:

∎ to return a purchase;

▌ to prove a date of purchase for a warranty-covered repair;

▌ to prove a purchase for tax purposes; and

▌ to reconcile a statement or bill.

How to deal with receipts

▌ Receipts saved to reconcile a statement or bill can be tossed out as soon as you reconcile the bill.

▌ Receipts saved in the event that you may return the item should be saved in an envelope marked "Receipts." Save receipts only for items worth over twenty dollars. You're unlikely to take the trouble to return items of a lesser value.

▌ Receipts for high-ticket items with warranty coverage such as appliances, electronics, housewares, or furniture should be kept, securely attached to the item itself, if possible, or in an envelope labeled "Receipts" with the present year's date on it.

▌ Receipts saved to document tax-deductible expenses should be saved in a tax folder, along with all other documents you gather throughout the year for preparation of tax returns.

Level Two Solutions:
Help from Friends and Family

Have Someone Else Pay Your Bills

The bills have to get paid somehow. If you tend to neglect bill paying because it's difficult for you, pass the job on to someone else! Another family member is fine. If you choose to go with an amateur bill payer like a family member, friend, or other person, their qualifications need to be trustworthiness, confidentiality, and the ability to do what it is you need. You'll still need to make yourself available to sign the checks.

If you want your finances kept strictly confidential, or you know no one personally who can pay your bills you can pay a bookkeeper or bill-paying service to do this for you. Bill-paying services and bookkeepers are listed in the yellow pages.

Use a Body Double

Financial organizing chores such as bill paying, balancing your checkbook, and analyzing financial statements are excellent opportunities to use a body double, someone who sits quietly with you while you attend to a financial organizing chore. Many people with ADD find that the calm presence of another person, who is there to keep them focused on their task, is very helpful. When you use a body double, the actual tasks of check writing and bill paying remain yours, but you might enlist your body double to perform small unobtrusive tasks such as sealing envelopes, affixing stamps, or doing filing. Your paper partner or a family member might make a good body double.

Level Three Solutions: Help from Professionals — Get Professional Help to Organize Your Financial Records

Some professional organizers specialize in financial organizing. Arrange for one to come in and help you set up your financial systems. A PO can also help you to regularly maintain your bill paying, financial filing, checkbook, and other financial chores.

Get Credit Counseling

If your credit card debt is more than 20 percent of your income, it's time to get more help. Contact a consumer credit counseling service. They can help put you on a budget, make regular payments, and protect your credit rating. They are listed in the phone book. If you are behind even one year in your taxes, get help. Call the IRS Consumer Assistance Program, listed in your phone book.

Working with a Coach to Learn ADD-Friendly Money Management

Mary's financial problems are not just related to paperwork. She struggles with out-of-control spending, too. Mary has tried to budget her money at various times with little success. Keeping a budget just adds to the financial record keeping that's so difficult for her. Mary needs an ADD-friendly approach to control her expenditures.

Move from Credit to Cash

Working with an ADD coach, the first step Mary takes is to destroy all of her credit cards and charge cards. Like many adults with ADD, she has difficulty tracking expenses that she has charged. As a result, her debts keep mounting. The new plan is to operate on a strict cash basis. When you deal on a cash basis, the reality of "can't afford it" becomes very concrete. With a charge card, there's too much room for living beyond your means.

Consolidate Debt

Mary and her ADD coach analyze her bills and her debts. On the advice of her coach, Mary speaks to a financial counselor. She consolidates her debts from various credit cards and charge accounts into a single monthly bill that can be managed on her income.

Prioritize Expenditures

She and her ADD coach calculate her other monthly expenses and considered her options. Mary has some tough choices to make. It is clear that she cannot continue to make car payments as well as pay the rent on her two-bedroom apartment. She has to sell her car, move to less expensive housing, or advertise for a roommate. Discussing her dilemma at work, a coworker mentions a friend who is searching for a roommate. Although reluctant to rent to a stranger, "A friend of a friend wouldn't be a *complete* stranger," Mary reasons. Mary meets with her and decides to rent her the second bedroom on a six-month trial basis.

Use Electronic Bill Paying

On the coach's advice, Mary contacts her bank to arrange for electronic bill paying. This eliminates her struggle with paying bills on time, managing paperwork, and balancing her bank account. Now all of this is handled through her bank.

Manage Daily Expenditures

With her monthly expenses reduced through her consolidation loan and a new roommate, Mary and her coach calculate how much money is left after all fixed expenses are paid each month. This figure becomes her "allowance" for *all* expenditures outside of her monthly bills.

The plan is to withdraw cash from an ATM machine twice a week, on Fridays and Mondays. Her Friday cash withdrawal gets her through the weekend. Another withdrawal on Monday lasts her through the work week.

Limit Access to Cash

To gain control of her spending, she resolves to never go to the ATM except at the preplanned times, withdrawing only preplanned amounts. To reduce the temptation to withdraw more, Mary sets up a special account for her ATM withdrawals. When her paycheck arrived at the bank on a bimonthly basis, she arranges for an automatic transfer into her "ATM account." The rest of her pay remains in the bill-paying account, to ensure that there is sufficient funds to cover her monthly bills.

Mary's cash allowance has to cover *all* purchases—groceries, gas, clothing, entertainment, and incidentals. If she gives in to an unplanned impulse purchase, Mary has to cut down on other purchases during the week by bringing her lunch from home, passing up casual purchases of nonessential items, and resisting clothes shopping. Mary soon gives up recreational shopping. On her strict budget, recreational shopping is self-inflicted torture—sort of like hanging out in front of the bakery when you're on a weight loss diet.

Make Choices

Managing her money on a cash basis is more concrete and understandable to Mary. She quickly learns to treat it like a challenging game. For example, when she wanted to buy expensive concert tickets, she plotted ways to cut down on groceries and incidentals—making a big pot of hearty soup that would last the week, for example. Having a cash allowance for all expenditures also has made her much more aware of purchases that she'd made previously with little or no thought. Before she had a set allowance, she just returned to the ATM when she ran out of cash. Now, however, she had clear, concrete limits on her spending without having to do complicated budgeting and recordkeeping—an ADD-friendly approach for managing her money.

Gain Control

For the first time since she left college, Mary feels in control of her finances. Future choices can be made realistically. When her parents offer her their older car, she jumps at the chance. Getting rid of the monthly car payment gives her money to buy clothes, or maybe even take a vacation next summer. For the first time, she is able to make concrete comparisons and prioritize her choices. She isn't drowning in paperwork, she isn't struggling with ADD-unfriendly record keeping. Instead her spending habits are under control.

Review

- Financial paperwork is an ADD-unfriendly activity.
- ADD increases financial anxiety.
- Math anxiety makes financial paperwork difficult.
- Organize your finances with the envelope bill-paying system and a bill-paying kit.
- The computer and the Internet can help you get your finances organized.
- The less "plastic" (charge cards) you use, the less paper you will have.
- Control receipt collecting.
- Hire someone to pay your bills for you.
- Take advantage of electronic bill paying.
- Consider using a body double for financial chores.
- A professional organizer can help you organize your financial records.
- Get credit counseling if you're in debt over your head.
- Work with an ADD coach to learn ADD-friendly money management.

Part Six

Conclusion

Putting Organizing Ideas into Action

Many issues have been covered in the preceding chapters, and many more organizing issues have been set aside. As authors, we chose the issues that we believe are most pressing for adults with ADD. We had to prioritize; we couldn't do it all. And that's exactly what you need to do as you begin to put the ideas in this book to work for you.

A typical pitfall that most adults with ADD experience is trying to do everything at once. Often, an adult seeks help for ADD, saying that they want to get control of their life. A laudable goal, but unreachable unless it is broken down into discrete parts that can be tackled one at a time.

So take heart as you begin to organize. Set small, doable goals. You'll build up steam by meeting those small goals. Success leads to confidence, and confidence leads to success.

Start Small

Don't choose your most overwhelming organizing task as a starting point. If your entire house is in disorder, choose a place to start that will bring the greatest satisfaction in the shortest amount of time. For example, if your feeling upon arriving home is one of being overwhelmed as you walk into a cluttered foyer, that may be a good place to begin. Probably, with a little focused effort, you can clear out your foyer in short order. Then, every time you come home, you'll feel heartened. "Doesn't this look nice!" That boost will encourage you to take on other organizing activities.

Remember, Organizing Is a Process, Not an Event

Consider your newly organized foyer, for example. Clearing it out may be a single, focused task, but keeping it that way is a process. Your foyer will start to become cluttered again, probably the very next day. At this point, you can begin a process of problem-solving. What's causing the clutter? Is the hall table too enticing a place to dump items as you enter the house with full hands? Maybe something as simple as removing the table will induce you to carry items to where they belong—or at least farther than the front foyer. Is the hall closet overfilled, leading you to hang your coat and scarf on the banister or tossed over the chair? Would you be more likely to hang coats in the closet if there were a greater supply of sturdy, accessible hangers? Problem-solving and taking action on the solutions you reach is part of the ongoing *process* of organizing.

Approach Organizing as You Would Juggling

When juggling, your goal is to juggle one ball, then two, then three, and so on. A juggler adds another ball only when he is capable of keeping all of them in the air. If your goal is to eventually have a clean, well-ordered home, start by juggling one ball (the foyer project). Don't pick up a second ball, such as organizing the family room, until you've got the first one down pat. You're not getting anywhere if you're juggling balls three, four, and five, but balls one and two have fallen back to the floor.

Can't Do It Alone? Then Do It Together!

Planning, initiating, and following through on good intentions are the types of activities that are difficult when you have ADD. This is not due to laziness or poor motivation. These tasks are difficult because, when you have ADD, the parts of the brain that are involved in planning and organizing are often unreliable and underaroused. Stimulant medication can help, but the structuring influence of other people cannot be overstated. The physical presence of another person, even if they are not lifting a finger to help you, can keep you focused on your task. Don't apologize for this need. Instead, recognize it and arrange your life accordingly. If you don't have friends or family members who can serve as organizing partners, use a PO or an ADD coach.

You might also consider finding an ADD organizing buddy; you can support one another in your organizing efforts. Although each of you may have difficulty organizing your own environment, you'll probably find that you're much more focused and effective in seeing what needs to be done in one another's cluttered environments. It's always easier to keep going when you have company and encouragement. Some adult ADD support groups are now organizing "dig-outs" of each others' home space. Many hands make light work, and being able to laugh over ADD foibles with others who *really do* understand can move you from self-criticism to self-acceptance.

Invest in the Professional Help You Need

Throughout this book, we write about ways to help yourself. We don't mean to imply, however, that you should *always* try to help yourself first. In fact, it may be best to begin with help from others—friends, family, or professionals.

In certain organizing or maintenance tasks, it may be best to routinely involve others. This is a critical aspect of creating an ADD-friendly lifestyle. Assess your strengths and weaknesses realistically, and engage the assistance of others, whenever possible, on tasks that are your areas of weakness. For example, consider having a professional organizer come into your home on a quarterly basis to organize your files and papers with you; or plan to have an accountant's assistant balance your checkbook and pay your bills on a monthly basis. Many people with ADD resist such advice, protesting, "I can't afford it." For some, this may be true, but perhaps you can barter services with a friend. When deciding whether support is affordable, it's essential to consider the cost of *not* enlisting support. The cost of going it alone may come in the form of missed deadlines, late fees on bills, a poor credit rating, missed deductions on tax returns, and time spent hunting for misplaced papers that could be spent earning money.

Reserve the "Crisis Mode" for Real Emergencies

Many people with ADD routinely create crises as motivators. As a daily mode of operation, this is exhausting and ineffective. A crisis mode of operation may be necessary from time to time, and may be necessary on a more frequent basis until you are further along in taking charge of your ADD. If your in-laws are arriving for a visit in three days, or the IRS has sent you an ominous letter, then perhaps your crisis mode is appropriate in the short run. But as much as you can, return to the "start small" maxim in your organizing efforts and stick to the *process* of building order in your life.

Be Realistic, Not Perfectionist

Disorganization is one of the greatest and most universal challenges for adults with ADD. While there are adults with ADD who are extremely organized, they typically pay a very high price, expending most of their waking energy to establish and maintain very rigid systems of organization. Many such people may appear to have obsessive compulsive disorder because they are hyperfocused on doing everything in a proscribed manner. Without this rigidity, their organizing systems fall apart.

Don't set such hyperorganization as your goal. It's a bit like becoming anorexic because you have a weight problem—a huge overcorrection that creates other problems. Perfectionism, like anorexia, can take over your life. Instead, aim for a level of organization that allows you to comfortably function in your daily life.

Maintain the "Right" Level of Focus

Adults with ADD can become caught in the "ant's view," concentrating on a single, sometimes unimportant, organizing activity while the rest of their world is falling apart. Often this hyperfocusing results from a need to reduce feelings of being overwhelmed. You may be able to manage "this one thing," but when you look at the whole mess you feel paralyzed. Others take a big-picture view, but can't focus on where to get started. Get familiar with your focusing tendencies, and try to become aware of when your level of focus is an organizing obstacle. The more flexible your level of focus, the greater your organizing success. Most organizing tasks require that you take a big-picture approach, set priorities, and move from one level to another, depending upon the demands of the task.

Don't Bite off More than You Can Chew

Many if not most adults with ADD have "eyes that are bigger than their bellies." They start off with the best intentions, and with great enthusiasm, underestimating how long things will take and how tiring the task will be. Then, when they become fatigued and discouraged, midtask, they are likely to abandon the project, resolving to finish it "later." Rather than surrounding yourself with discouraging, half-completed or never-completed projects, try to "underdo it." Pick only a portion of your closet to organize. If you still have energy, after you reorganize the shelves at one end of your closet, there's nothing to stop you from taking on another minitask, such as sorting and organizing the shoes on your closet floor.

Remind Yourself

Throughout this book, we introduced many tips, ADD-friendly strategies, and maxims. You've probably tried to build new habits in the past without much success. Instead, try reminding yourself about the new habit you're trying to develop. If there is a particular idea or strategy that you're trying to build as a habit, write it large on a piece of paper and place it where you'll see it often. That's a good way to work *with* your ADD as you organize your life.

Be a Model for Your Children

You may not have had the benefit of knowing that you had ADD when you were growing up. As you work hard to better understand yourself and ways to take charge of your life, you can help your children to avoid many of the struggles that you have experienced. One invaluable gift that you can give your children is to serve as a role model, teaching them by example how to create an ADD-friendly life that allows you to take charge of your ADD and live up to your potential.

You can show them, by example, how to lower the stress level in their lives and how to manage the many activities and responsibilities of life. Time-management skills are among the most important skills to develop, but they are rarely taught in school. At home, however, your children can *see* you learning how to better manage your time—writing a to-do list, consulting your calendar, and keeping an ongoing list of projects.

If you are an adult with ADD who is raising a child with ADD, learning the time-management skills described in Part IV and implementing these skills in your daily life will teach your child that these are the habits that people develop to manage their lives well. Our children are much more apt to imitate what we *do* than what we *say*. So instead of nagging your child to write down homework assignments and remember to do chores, show your child, by example, how you manage the same issues in your own life. Better yet, why not work on developing new habits together? Allowing your child to see you set goals, make mistakes, try again, and make progress—even allowing your child to help you track your own progress toward your goal—can make habit development an ADD-friendly family activity.

In Conclusion

Choose a doable task to begin your reorganization and use the maxims and instructions you've chosen as your guidelines for getting started. Remember, start small and finish what you start. Organizing is an ongoing process, not a time-limited activity. Build habits, solve organizing problems creatively, and give yourself permission to get the help you need from others. You'll get there, creating an organized ADD-friendly life one step at a time!

Part *Seven*

Resources

Organizing Resources

Products

These companies offer organizing products useful for organizing time, tasks, paper, clutter, and storage areas. Most will send you a catalogue.

ABBOT OFFICE SYSTEM
5012 Asbury Ave.
Farmingdale, NJ 07727
(800) 631-2233
Fax 732-938-4419

CARDINAL BRANDS
12312 Olive Blvd., Suite 400
St. Louis, MO 63141
www.cardinalbrands.com

THE CONTAINER STORE
2000 Valwood Parkway
Dallas, TX 75234-8800
1-800-786-7315
www.containerstore.com

ELDON
2514 Fish Hatchery Road
Madison, WI 53713-2407
608-257-2227
www.eldonoffice.com

ESSELTE
48 S. Service Road, Suite 400
Melville, NY 11747-2340
631-675-5700
www.esselte.com

FELLOWES MANUFACTURING CO.
1789 Norwood Avenue
Itasca, IL 60143
1-800-945-4545
www.fellowes.com

GET ORGANIZED
600 Cedar Hollow Road
Malvern, PA 19355
1-800-803-9400
www.getorginc.com

LILLIAN VERNON
100 Lillian Vernon Drive
Virginia Beach, VA 23479-0002
1-800-505-2250
www.lillianvernon.com

ORGANIZE-IT
133 S. Livernois Road
Rochester Hills, MI 48307
1-800-210-7712
www.organizes-it.com

RUBBERMAID HOME PRODUCTS
1147 Akron Road
Wooster, OH 44691-6000
Attn: Consumer Services
www.newellco.com

SMEAD MANUFACTURING CO.
600 Smead Blvd.
Hastings, MN 55033-2219
651-437-4111
www.smead.com

Organizing Time

CRISP LEARNING
1200 Hamilton Court
Menlo Park, CA 94025-1427
1-800-442-7477
Fax 1-650-323-5800
www.crisp.com

EZ-POCKET
1191 South Yosemite Way
Suite 47
Denver, CO 80231
1-800-681-8681
Fax 303-671-5477
ezpocket@ezpocket.com

TIME TIMER, INC.
7707 Camargo Road
Cincinnati, OH 45243
1-887-771-TIME
513-561-2599
Fax 513-561-4699
www.timetimer.com

Organizing Paper

20th CENTURY DIRECT
P.O. Box 2393
Brea, CA 92822-2393
1-800-767-0777
www.20thcenturydirect.com

NEWELL OFFICE PRODUCTS
6833 Statler Drive
Rockford, IL 61108
1-800-446-5652
www.newellco.com

Books and Audio Tapes

Aslett, Don. *Clutter Free, Finally and Forever.* Cincinnati, OH: Betterway Publishers, 1995.

Culp, Stephanie. *How to Conquer Clutter.* Cincinnati, OH: F&W Publications, 1989.

Felton, Sandra. *When You Live with a Messie.* Old Tappan, NJ: Fleming H. Revell, 1994.

Felton, Sandra. *The Whiz Bang Guide on How to Organize Time and Things.* Messies Anonymous, 1-800-MESS-AWAY (1-800-637-7292).

Kolberg, Judith. *Conquering Chronic Disorganization.* Atlanta: Squall Press, 1998, (404-289-1622).

Kolberg, Judith. *Surviving Chronic Disorganization.* Atlanta: Squall Press, 1999. (404-289-1622)

McGee-Cooper, Ann. *Time Management For Unmanageable People.* Dallas: Bowen, 1993.

Morgenstern, Julie. *Organizing From the Inside Out.* New York: Henry Holt, 1998.

Organizing Resources

Groups and Organizations

American Coaching Association

P.O. Box 353
Lafayette Hill, PA 19444
610-825-4505
Fax 610-825-4505
susansussman@compuserve.com

Messies Anonymous

5025 SW 114 Ave.
Miami, Florida 33165
www.messiesanonymous.com

Finding a Professional Organizer

National Association of Professional Organizers

P.O. Box 140647
Austin, TX 78714-0647
512-454-8626
www.napo.net

National Study Group on Chronic Disorganization

P.O. Box 1990
Elk Grove, CA 95759
916-962-6227
www.nsgd@nsgcd.org

Finding an ADD Coach

There are many websites relating to ADD coaching. Some of the most established ADD coaching organizations include:

- www.americoach.org
- www.nancyratey.com
- www.addcoaching.com

ADD Resources

Books and Other Publications

AD/HD Report. Russell Barkley, Ed. New York: Guilford Press. 800-365-7006.
A bimonthly newsletter for professionals with articles and reviews of recent research.

Additude. Ellen Kingsley, Ed.www.additudemag.com.
A monthly general-circulation magazine about AD/HD in children, teens, and adults.

ADDvance News Online. Kathleen Nadeau and Patricia Quinn, Eds. www.ncgiadd.org.
A monthly electronic newsletter including articles and review of research pertaining to women and girls with AD/HD.

Hallowell, Ned, & Ratey, John. (1994). *Driven to Distraction.* New York: Pantheon.

Nadeau, Kathleen. (1996). *Adventures in Fast Forward.* New York: Brunner/Mazel.

Nadeau, Kathleen. (1997). *ADD in the Workplace.* New York: Brunner/Mazel.

Nadeau, Kathleen, & Quinn, Patricia. (Eds.). (2002). *Understanding Women with AD/HD.* Silver Spring, MD: Advantage Books.

Quinn, Patricia, & Kathleen Nadeau (Eds.). (2002). *Gender Issues and AD/HD.* Silver Spring, MD: Advantage Books.

Solden, Sari. (1995). *Women with Attention Deficit Disorder.* Grass Valley, CA: Underwood.

ADD Groups and Other Publications

ADDA

The National Attention Deficit Disorder Association is a nonprofit advocacy organization that focuses more on issues of teens and adults. Membership includes a bimonthly newsletter, *Focus,* and discounts at the annual national meeting.

1788 Second Street, Suite 200
Highland Park, IL 60035
847-432-5874
www.add.org

CHADD

National advocacy organization for children and adults with ADD, CHADD has a highly informative website with scientifically accurate information as well as an online bookstore. For CHADD support groups near you, check the map on the website. Membership includes a monthly magazine. CHADD holds a national conference and several regional conferences yearly.

8181 Professional Place, Suite 201
Landover, MD 20785
800-233-4050
Fax 301-306-7090
www.chadd.org

National Center for Gender Issues and AD/HD

A nonprofit organization that focuses on AD/HD issues of women and girls. Membership includes *ADDvance News Online,* a monthly electronic newsletter, a discount on books sold on their website, and discounts to events and conferences sponsored by the National Center.

2001 Spring Street, Suite 206
Silver Spring, MD 20910
888-238-8588
www.ncgiadd.org

About the Authors

Judith Kolberg is a graduate of the State University of New York at Binghamton with a degree in sociology. She came to the south in 1986 as a professional political organizer, working on campaigns and lobbying efforts associated with independent politics. In 1989 she founded her consulting business, FileHeads Professional Organizers. To address the special organizing needs of chronically disorganized adults, Kolberg founded the National Study Group on Chronic Disorganization in 1992 and served as its director for seven years. She counts many ADD adults in her client base. Kolberg is the author of *Conquering Chronic Disorganization* (Squall Press) and is a recipient of the prestigious Founder's Award from the National Association of Professional Organizers. She is a master trainer in the area of chronic disorganization and is currently a knowledge-management consultant in Atlanta.

Kathleen Nadeau, Ph.D., is a clinical psychologist and the director of the Chesapeake Center for Attention and Learning in Silver Spring, Maryland. Author of numerous books on ADD for children, teens, college students, and adults, she is a frequent lecturer on ADD both nationally and internationally. The major emphasis in her clinical work, her writing, and her lectures is on practical, life-management strategies for ADD that help individuals to take charge of their lives and reach their potential.

Index

Index